PROBLEMS
OF
MIND AND MATTER

PROBLEMS
OF
MIND AND MATTER

BY

JOHN WISDOM

Professor of Philosophy in the University of Cambridge

CAMBRIDGE
AT THE UNIVERSITY PRESS
1970

130.1
W811

PUBLISHED BY
THE SYNDICS OF THE CAMBRIDGE UNIVERSITY PRESS

Bentley House, 200 Euston Road, London, N.W. 1
American Branch: 32 East 57th Street, New York 22, N.Y.

ISBN O 521 08508 X

First printed	1934
First paperback edition	1963
Reprinted	1970

First printed in Great Britain at the University Press, Cambridge
Reprinted in the United States of America

PREFACE TO
THE PAPERBACK EDITION

This book is clear, correct, cogent and boring except for a few places where it is not clear and correct. This makes it, unlike the charge of the Light Brigade at Balaclava, an instructive failure. That the charge would fail anyone could see before the horses reached a trot. It is said that a Frenchman watching the Brigade advance said 'C'est magnifique, mais ce n'est pas la guerre'. When I was a child and this remark was translated for me I still could not understand why grown up people regarded it as worth attention. It is incorrect. No attempt to prove it could be cogent. Its contradictory is correct.

Consider the following propositions: (1) Mathematics is magnificent but it isn't knowledge. (2) History is magnificent but it isn't knowledge. (3) All our so called knowledge of the minds of others isn't knowledge. (4) All our so called knowledge of material things isn't knowledge. In the case of each of these propositions one may notice that its contradictory is correct and that therefore any argument for it must involve a *non sequitur*. Anyone who as soon as he has noticed this gives no more attention to these propositions or the arguments which have been adduced for them will do as little philosophy as I do in *Problems of Mind and Matter*.

For he will do nothing towards bringing to light that variety in the modes of knowledge which our habitual, normal, correct application of the concept of knowledge conceals.

The same desire to say only what is correct will make him dismiss, as I do in my book, all philosophical proposition of the sort 'Statements about minds are analysable into statements about material things' or 'Statements about material things are analysable into statements about minds'.

While we say only what's correct we shall not say what's incorrect. But we may then fail to see much that we might have seen.

MARCH 1963   JOHN WISDOM

PREFACE

In this book an attempt is made to give an elementary but not too inaccurate introduction to the applications in philosophy of what is now sometimes called the analytic method. This might have been done by explaining the nature of analysis, but here little is said *about* analysis and instead elementary examples of its *use* are given.

Foolishly, perhaps, but only occasionally, the bearing of the analysis upon certain speculative theories has been suggested.

How much of this book is dependent upon Professor G. E. Moore's work will be obvious. The definition of mental facts (p.15) and the analysis of perception (Part II) are his (apart from inaccuracies). The philosophic part of the discussion of the relation between body and mind is based upon Professor G. F. Stout's book *Mind and Matter*. In the interpretation of this book I have received great help from conversation with Professor Stout and Mr Alec Mace and from Professor C. D. Broad's critical notice of it in *Mind*.

I thank Miss Helen Smith, Professor L. S. Stebbing and Professor Broad for the help and encouragement they have given me.

J. W.

Cambridge
July 1934

CONTENTS

CONTENTS

PART I

BODY AND MIND

CONTENTS

CONTENTS

CONTENTS

PART II

COGNITION

xiii

CONTENTS

xv

INTRODUCTION

1. **Analysis and Speculative Philosophy.** It is to analytic philosophy that this book is intended to be an introduction. Consequently it is not concerned with certain questions which are properly called 'philosophical'. Philosophers have asked whether God exists, whether good or ill prevails, whether men are immortal, whether the world is in spite of appearances merely material, and whether in spite of appearances it is wholly spiritual and a unity. These speculative questions are clearly a great deal more important than questions of the analytic kind which have also been asked by philosophers, such questions as "What is the ultimate nature of the soul?"; "What is the ultimate nature of matter, time and space?". The speculative questions are the more important because, if they could be answered, we should thereby obtain new information about matters which concern us very much, while the answering of analytic questions does not provide us with knowledge of new facts but only with clearer knowledge of facts already known. To learn, or, better, to come to see clearly, the ultimate nature of the soul is to come to see clearly how facts about the soul which are known already are constituted—what their elements are and how they are arranged. Occasionally an analytic result bears upon a speculative theory, but to remember this only prejudices one's analysis. Speculating and analysing are operations which differ in kind; the object of the one is truth,

I

the object of the other is clarity. It is with the latter that we shall be concerned.

An introduction to a science, such as chemistry, will contain a selection of the easier and more fundamental chemical truths. In my opinion there cannot be such an introduction to analytic philosophy. For there is no special set of analytic truths. Analytic philosophy has no special subject-matter. You can philosophise about Tuesday, the pound sterling, and lozenges and philosophy itself. This is because the analytic philosopher, unlike the scientist, is not one who learns new truths, but one who gains new insight into old truths. In a sense, philosophy cannot be taught—any more than one can teach riding or dancing or musical appreciation. However, philosophers can be made. They can be made in two ways, namely by practice and by precept. The first method is the one usually adopted by lecturers in philosophy or performing philosophers. They themselves perform philosophic antics in front of their students, interlarded with anecdotes about the antics of contemporary performers. This is called giving a course in modern philosophy. Or, they tell stories about performers of the past: then they are giving a course in the history of philosophy. Sometimes their students are able to imitate these performances; they are the 'good students'. The second method of making philosophers, namely, the precept method, has not been much used. This is because even good philosophers have been confused about what it is they are trying to do, and have been, like many good riders, unable to say what it is about their methods which makes them good. In this book I shall rely almost wholly upon the first method. My performance will (I trust) give the reader some idea of what the goal of the analytic philosopher is and how it is reached. I can, of course, say here and now that (i) the goal of the analytic philosopher is insight into facts; and that (ii) insight is clear apprehension of the ultimate structure of facts; and that (iii) the structure of a fact is clearly apprehended when one apprehends clearly the form, the elements, and the arrangement of the elements of that fact.

Instead of trying to define these expressions let us consider one or two examples of analysis. We may begin with the definition of 'history', 'science', 'mental facts' and 'material facts'. To define 'science' will bring out the distinction between the goal of the scientist and the goal of the philosopher. To define 'mental' and 'material' is important because confusion between the two is at once easy and peculiarly fatal in philosophy. In defining 'science' and 'mental facts' we shall arrive at a definition of 'psychology' because psychology is the science of mental facts.

2. **First Examples of Analysis.** Psychology is made up of psychological science and psychological history. For part of psychology is a natural science, seeking causal laws, like chemistry and physics and the kind of economics found in Marshall's *Principles of Economics*. And part of psychology is historical, tracing developments, like economic history and theories of the development of complicated organisms from simple ones.

To define 'psychological history' one must consider

3

first what is meant by calling it 'history' and then what is meant by calling it 'psychological'. And the same two problems will arise in connexion with the definition of psychological science. We will begin by finding rough definitions of 'history' and 'science' and then we will consider the significance of the word 'psychological'.

2.1. HISTORY. There are reasons why it would be better not to call history a science at all. The story of a single person, an autobiography, is not called a scientific work but a work of art. And though the history of many people provides a better illustration of the laws of science than does the history of one person, such a history should still be called art rather than science. For the historian is a story-teller. The historian however differs from the ordinary story-teller in two ways. (i) If any part of the historian's story is 'tall' then he tries to provide evidence for it. (ii) He not only says that first these particular events occurred and then those; he also tries to say which caused what. Thus on p. 10 of *Landmarks in English Industrial History* Mr Townsend Warner writes "Stock-and-land leases were not indeed unknown before the Black Death, but the agricultural crisis which ensued from it gave a great impulse to their adoption, for they held out real advantages to both sides".

Now just as part of economics is the story and explanation of how the present complicated economic world developed from a simpler economic world, so part of psychology is the story and explanation of how the present complicated psychological world developed from

4

a simpler psychological world. Thus economic history traces the development of methods of exchange from barter to cheques; psychological history tries to trace the development of thinking from the simple sort of thinking which occurs when there is no language to the more complex sort of thinking which becomes possible when language is used. This is what Professor Stout does in his chapter in *The Groundwork of Psychology* on the development of language. And McDougall tries to trace the development of moral judgments in his *Introduction to Social Psychology*, chapters VII and VIII. Psychological history is usually called *genetic* psychology.

Psychological history differs from economic history in *degree* in two ways. (*a*) The economic historian knows from good evidence the nature of the simpler economic world from which the present one has developed. The psychological historian, on the other hand, is obliged to make guesses, supported by analogy with animals and children, as to the nature of the simpler psychological world from which the present one has developed. (*b*) The causal laws which the economist can use to explain the sequence of economic events are many and clear. The causal laws which the psychologist uses to explain the sequence of psychological events are few and muddled. So much for psychological history. We must now try to say something about psychological causal laws—the scientific part of psychology.

2.2. SCIENCE. Every scientific law is concerned with causation. But we cannot define a scientific law as a fact concerned with causation. For a fact about a particular event that it caused another particular event is not a law of science. *The 'Speenhamland Act' of the Berkshire justices in* 1795 *caused the subsequent idleness and thriftlessness among the poor of that time* and *Henry VIII was annoyed by Wolsey's opposition* are both facts concerned with causation; yet neither is a law of science. This is because each of these two facts, though causal, is not universal. Each is particular, since each is concerned with the causal relations between one particular event and another. An event, properly speaking, is always particular in that it involves the state of certain things throughout a certain region of space throughout a certain period of time. Thus the 'Speenhamland Act' was an event in Speenhamland in 1795 consisting in certain people, the Berkshire justices, declaring that outdoor relief should be given. And the subsequent poverty involved particular people at a particular time and place. Hence we call the fact that the 'Act' caused the poverty a *particular* fact. For by a 'particular fact' is meant a fact which is about a particular person or thing, place and time; and a fact which is about the relationship between one particular event and another must be concerned with particular things, places and times. A law of science, on the other hand, is universal; for, though it governs events, it never mentions any particular event, such as Nebuchadnezzar's dream of the golden image, but only classes of events. For example, *All dreams are caused by unfulfilled wishes* would be, if true, a law of science. Hence a law of science does not mention particular things (or persons), places or times.

2.21. A law of science is a *universal* causal fact. A universal causal fact is a fact to the effect that every event of such and such a kind, no matter what particular things, times and places it involves, always causes an event of such and such another kind. For example, the following are both causal laws: *Always and everywhere anyone who gives outdoor relief causes idleness and thriftlessness in anyone to whom he gives it* and *Always and everywhere an event which consists in one person's opposing another will cause an event which consists in the other's annoyance with the one*. Neither mentions any particular thing, time or place; each mentions only certain qualities and relations, and states that an event consisting in the presence throughout any region of space and time of such and such qualities and relations will cause the presence of such and such other qualities and relations.

2.22. A law of science is a *generic* universal causal fact. Even when the scientist has learned a number of universal causal facts he is still dissatisfied; he wishes to find generic universal facts from which special universal facts may be deduced. This is because he wishes to find the smallest number of laws which will explain any sequence of particular events. Suppose that by using a great many universal but not very general laws (rules of thumb) the scientist is able to predict and explain particular events. Obviously if he can find a few general laws from which his multitude of special laws can be deduced, then he will be able to predict with these few general laws all that he was able to predict and explain by means of the many special laws, and usually a great deal more besides. Thus suppose I know both that taking mustard and that taking a warm drink cause sleep. Then I can explain why Charles sleeps after beef sandwiches but not after mutton, and why he sleeps after an evening at his grandmother's (she provides Ovaltine) but not after an evening at the Club. But I shall be at a loss to know why he sleeps when at home but not when he stays at a hotel. Now suppose that I learn that anything which draws excess blood from the head promotes sleep. Then I can explain not only all that I could explain before, but also why Charles sleeps when at home (with a hot-water bottle) and not when at a hotel (without the hot-water bottle). For the laws about mustard and warm drinks follow from the more general law concerning blood in the head, together with laws about the action of mustard and warmth upon the blood stream. And, in addition, there follows a law about hot-water bottles. Again, we have all been told that once when an apple fell near Newton the explanation of this occurrence dawned on him. In what sense is this true? Long before Newton there were people who could explain up to a point the falling of the apple. These people would have said, "The stalk of the apple broke, and unsupported bodies fall to earth". Presumably then Newton's advance on these people consisted in his showing that the law—*Lack of support causes fall to earth*—is a special case of, and thus deducible from, more general laws. Newton saw that the fact that unsupported bodies fall to earth was a special case of the law of gravity which may be inexactly stated in the form *Any two material things tend to approach one another*.

2.23. A law of science is an *exact* general universal causal fact. Even when the scientist has found causal facts which are not only universal but also generic, he is still dissatisfied. For he seeks knowledge which is not merely universal and generic, but also exact. He is interested in the fact that you fell when your horse did, only as evidence for the universal fact that everyone falls when his horse does; and he is interested in this universal fact only as a special case of the more generic fact that unsupported bodies fall; and he is interested in this generic and universal fact only as a special case of the still more generic fact that material things approach one another. All this we have seen already. Now we must add that the scientist is interested in the highly generic universal causal fact that material things approach one another, only as an approximation to the *exact* law that material things approach one another with an acceleration inversely proportional to the square of the distance.[1]

To sum up: The historian relates in order particular facts and tries to trace causal connexions between these particular facts. The scientist seeks causal facts which are (a) universal, (b) generic, and (c) exact.

The tasks of the historian and the scientist are to some extent interdependent. The historian cannot provide his explanations of particular facts without the scientist's laws; the scientist may find the historian's story of the order of particular facts suggestive of universal facts; and the test of the scientist's suggestions as to

[1] I have neglected differences of mass.

9

what are the laws of nature is their success in predicting the course of nature, that is, the sequence of particular facts.

So much for the respects in which one kind of historian resembles another and one kind of scientist resembles another. Next we must see how one kind of historian differs from another and one kind of scientist differs from another.

The political historian differs from the economic historian in the kind of particular fact with which he deals; and the chemist differs from the physicist in the kind of particular fact with which he deals, that is in the kind of particular fact which his laws govern. To put it briefly: Branches of history agree in point of *form* but differ in point of *material*. Branches of science agree in point of *form* and differ in *field of application*. If we agree to mean by 'subject-matter' *either* 'material' (facts recounted), *or* 'field of application' (facts governed), we may say: Different branches of history and of science agree in form but differ in subject-matter. It follows that to define a 'psychologist' we need now to know only one more thing—his subject-matter. For to know this will enable us to distinguish the psychological historian from all other historians and the psychological scientist from all other scientists.

2.3. MENTAL FACTS. The kind of particular facts with which the psychologist deals are particular *mental* facts. In order to frame a definition of mental facts let us consider a list of examples:

(*a*) He feels pleased.

(*b*) He sees that this table is larger than that.

(*c*) He imagines himself in a castle in Spain.

(*d*) He conceives Space to be infinite.

(*e*) He wishes he were in a castle in Spain.

(*f*) He believes in fairies.

(*g*) He dreamed of reindeer.

(*h*) Forgetting his own existence and desires for this and that, he watched it pass.

(*i*) That flag frightened your horse.

(*j*) Satan is annoyed.

It is clear from these examples that every mental fact involves a mind, though this mind may be that of an animal, see (*i*) above, or an unembodied spirit (*j*). But this does not take us very far. For the expression 'a mind' is even more obscure than the expression 'a mental fact'.

Every fact in the above list is a case either of feeling somehow (*a*); or of awareness of something, either by perceiving (*b*), or imagining (*c*), or conceiving (*d*); or a combination of the two (*e*) and (*i*). A mental fact then is a case of feeling somehow, or of awareness of something, or of both. This suggests a more generic description still. For both feeling and awareness imply consciousness, while consciousness implies either feeling or awareness or both. Hence we may write: A particular mental fact is one of the kind *This person is conscious in such and such a way now*. Thus *He is watching it now* is a particular mental fact. Of course *He was watching it then* is also a particular mental fact, so that strictly our definition of a particular mental fact should run: A particular mental fact is one of the kind *This person is (was, will be) conscious in such and such a way now (then)*. Or, remembering the definition of 'particular fact', we might write: A particular mental fact is a particular fact involving consciousness.

Clearly the important words in the above definitions are 'conscious' and 'consciousness'. No examiner would think much of my answer above to the question "What is the subject-matter of psychology?" if it were not completed by an explanation of the use of the word 'conscious' in the above definitions. For the word 'conscious' is ambiguous; that is, some people mean one thing by it and other people mean something else. Consequently, if I use the word I convey nothing definite by it until I explain in which of its several senses I am using it.

I cannot analyse what I mean by 'conscious', but I want to make known to you what I attribute to a thing when I call it 'conscious'. When using the word in this special sense I will write it *conscious*. And I will now set down the clues to what I mean by *conscious*.

(i) *Conscious* implies *either feels or is aware*.

(ii) Consider the change which comes over a man as he comes round from chloroform or from *dreamless* sleep. You know quite well the kind of change I mean. That kind of change I call 'becoming *conscious*'. Of course as you come round from chloroform all sorts of *bodily* changes are taking place—the nerves are recovering from the chemical poison; and as you come round from sleep more blood flows to the brain. So that, strictly, there is nothing that can be called '*the* change' which takes place when one comes round from chloroform and sleep. Nevertheless, these bodily changes are not the ones you thought of when I spoke of *the* change; you never thought of blood and brain. That kind of change which you immediately thought of when I spoke of the change from sleep or chloroform, is the one I express by 'becoming *conscious*'.

(iii) *Conscious* does not mean *alive*. A tree is alive but not conscious. An amœba is certainly alive yet quite likely not conscious.

(iv) *Conscious* does not mean *living and sensitive*. A man in a dreamless sleep is a living and sensitive being; but he is not at that time conscious in my sense, i.e. *conscious*. Of course such a man is conscious compared with a tree or a dead man; more accurately there is *a* sense of 'conscious' in which it is correct to say that he is a conscious being. He is conscious in the derived and hypothetical sense that, if he were shaken, he would become *conscious* (fundamental sense).

This hypothetical sense of 'conscious' is less fundamental than that in terms of which mental facts are to be defined, that is *conscious*. For 'conscious' (in this hypothetical sense) has a meaning derived from, i.e. defined in terms of, *conscious*. In other words, if we split up the meaning of the hypothetical sense, we find that one of its elements is *conscious*. It is easy to see that this is so. '*S* is conscious' (in the sense in which this is true even when he is in a dreamless sleep) means "If you shook *S* he would become conscious". Now 'conscious' on the right-hand side of the equation cannot be used in the very way it is on the left. For then we shall have '*S* is con-

scious' = "If you shook S he would become conscious"
= "If you shook S he would become such that if you
shook him he would become conscious" and so on without end. Such a series is a vicious infinite generated by
trying to make the hypothetical meaning of 'conscious'
an element of itself. There is no objection to a *different*
sense of 'conscious', namely *conscious*, being an element
of the hypothetical sense. And it is now clear that this
in fact is so. That is 'conscious' (hypothetical sense or
sense number 2) is derived from *conscious*. This is what
we wished to show. We have seen that "S is *conscious*"
does not mean "S is alive" and it does not mean "S is a
conscious being", i.e. "S is conscious in the hypothetical
sense that, if he were stimulated he would become *conscious*". And these two points are vividly brought out
if we remember that a man *becomes conscious* as he wakes
from dreamless sleep. For a person still in a dreamless
sleep is nevertheless alive and a conscious being.

(v) S is *conscious* implies neither (1) that S is conscious
of his environment nor (2) that S is conscious of himself.
As to (1), a man is *conscious* when he is dreaming (see (g)
in list) and therefore when unconscious of his environment. I do not deny, on the contrary I assert, that there
is *a* usual and therefore perfectly respectable sense in
which 'conscious' is used, which *does* imply 'conscious
of his environment'. Thus, when we say "Is he conscious?", meaning "Has he regained consciousness?"
(after an accident), we *do* mean "Is he now again conscious *of his environment*?" But it will be seen that this
third way of using 'conscious' is yet another sense derived from our first, that is, the sense we write *conscious*.

For 'conscious' (sense 3) means '*conscious* of environment'.

As to (2), a man may be conscious and yet be unconscious of himself (see (i) in list of mental facts above). It is important to add clause (2) because some psychologists use 'conscious' in a sense which implies consciousness of self. Thus they would deny that animals are conscious, because, although they would admit that dogs smell bones and are therefore *conscious*, they would deny that a dog ever thinks to himself, "*I* shall do so and so", e.g. "take that bone". In other words, they deny that an animal is ever *conscious* of itself and they express their view very misleadingly by saying that animals are not conscious. This fourth sense of 'conscious' is obviously also derived from *conscious*. So we may write:

(vi) *Conscious* is the fundamental sense of 'conscious' —that is the sense in terms of which all other senses are defined.

So much for the sense of 'conscious' which we require. A particular mental fact is a fact about a particular thing at a particular time to the effect that it is *conscious* or *conscious* in such and such a specific way, e.g. is unpleasantly *conscious* of the motion of this ship.

We can now define a 'psychologist'. He is one who either seeks causal laws governing particular mental facts, e.g. *Dreams are caused by unfulfilled wishes*; or seeks an account of the way in which this world, containing complicated particular mental facts, has developed from a world containing only simpler particular mental facts.

We must add that psychology, like economics, contains also an analytic part. An analytic psychologist defines kinds of particular mental fact. Thus, just as the analytic economist seeks to define 'wealth', 'income', 'rent', so does the analytic psychologist seek to define 'belief', 'decision' and 'love'.

Analytic psychology is not very fashionable at present. It is asserted that it "is no good". You will find out, on enquiry from the people who say this, that they mean that analytic psychology "has no practical importance". Now "has no practical importance" means here "leads to no good other than itself", i.e. "is not useful". When the objection to analytic psychology is thus plainly stated, it is a good deal less frightening. For (*a*) a thing may be well worth doing even if it leads to no further good, for example auction bridge and Beethoven. And (*b*) even this milder accusation, namely that analytic psychology is useless, is false. Those who call analytic psychology useless generally assert and often exaggerate the utility of the scientific part of psychology. Now the scientific part is useful because it enables us to predict and prevent fatigue, neurosis, etc. And it enables us to do this because it consists of causal laws. We have seen that a causal law asserts a causal connexion between one kind of particular fact and another. How can we learn whether one kind of fact, e.g. manic-depressive disorder, is caused in this way or that, unless we can distinguish the fact with which we are concerned from others, e.g. schizophrenia? But to distinguish the one from the other is to do analytic psychology.

There is a good deal of excuse for those who think ill of analytic psychology. Analytic psychologists, that is those psychologists who have much concerned themselves with analytic psychology, have mixed up historical, scientific and analytic problems to a shocking degree. This has given the impression that they believe all their analysis to be a necessary preliminary to the establishing of psychological laws. This is very far from being so. The analysis of the self, of the perception of material things, of the relation of each mind to its body, these are problems of *philosophical* analysis and quite unnecessary for science.[1] The psychologist, it is true, constantly talks about selves or persons; and it may be that persons can be analysed into clusters of mental and bodily states in the way that nations can be analysed into the individuals which are said to belong to those nations. Whenever we say anything about a nation, for example that it is a monarchy, we are only saying something, though not quite the same thing, about its nationals, for example that they all own the same man as king. Perhaps whenever we speak about a person we are in the same way just saying something about the set of states which we usually describe as belonging to him. But the psychologist need not ask whether persons and animals are or are not analysable in this sense; much less need he ask what that analysis is. It is quite certain that facts are expressed with the help of the words 'persons' and 'animals', and these words are not ambiguous; conse-

[1] Here I exaggerate. Philosophical analysis up to a point is sometimes useful in science. Thus the philosophical analysis of instincts, the unconscious, Freud's censor, may be useful. But there is no need to carry it to the length of analysing persons, animals and material things.

quently any hearer knows quite well what fact is being expressed by any speaker who uses the words. This is almost all the scientist needs and what more he needs is provided by *material* analysis, i.e. analytic definition, i.e. the setting out of the connotation of an expression.

The analytic definition of belief, memory, instinct, etc., removes ambiguity, and, at the same time, when the words defined present to the mind several facts at once, presents them separately. Thus, when we define "*A* is in awe of *B*" by "*A* fears and admires *B*", we present separately the two relations between *A* and *B* which are presented but not separately by "*A* is in awe of *B*". This separate presentation is often useful when the causes of mental states are being sought. For sometimes one of the states which a complex state contains is caused in one way while the other state which it contains is caused in another. This would be true for example of awe. Thus analytic definition may well be very important to science.

2.4. MATERIAL FACTS. I give below a list of examples of material facts.

(α) This is round.
(β) This adjoins that.
(γ) This is red.
(δ) This is smooth.
(ε) This is cool.
(ζ) This is a table.
(η) This table is larger than that.

You will see at once that each material fact implies that something has size, that something is spread out in space. A particular material fact corresponds to an event which occupies not only time but also space. Thus movement and blushing both occupy space. Now mental events occupy time but they do not occupy space. One patch of colour may be larger than another but the perception of the one is not larger than the perception of the other. *Size* and *shape* do not apply to perceptions and beliefs.

You will notice also that there are two importantly different kinds of material fact. Nothing can be red without having size; for red is a quality which is manifested only in being spread throughout an area. It *can* not be manifested otherwise. This is true also of *cool*, *hard* and *smooth*. Let us express this by calling these qualities *extensive* qualities. A fact to the effect that a thing has such and such an extensive quality we may call an *extensive material fact*. Besides saying what colour or temperature is manifested throughout an area, we may say what size that area has, and what shape it has, and how far and in what direction other areas are from it. (See α and β.) Let us call these characters *spatial* characters. A fact to the effect that a thing has such and such a spatial character we may call a *spatial material fact*.

A particular material fact is a fact with regard to a particular thing that it has such and such an extensive quality or that it has such and such a spatial quality, or it is some combination of such facts. (For complex material facts see (ζ) and (η).)

He observes that this table is larger than that is a mental fact which contains a material fact. It is not itself a material fact, since it is not with regard to something to the effect that it has an extensive quality or a spatial quality.[1]

3. **Analytic Vocabulary.** It will be well at this point to introduce certain technical expressions without which it would be very difficult to do philosophy.

3.1. COMPONENTS AND CONSTITUENTS. In this book the word 'fact' will be used often, but in no unusual way, so that it will not be a source of difficulty. The *Strand Magazine* often uses the word 'fact' and nobody makes any bother; in this book the word will be used in those ways in which it is used in the *Strand*.[2]

[1] See App. 1.

[2] (*a*) I do not assume that the *Strand* always uses 'fact' in the same way. I believe that 'fact' has many uses (see "Logical Constructions", *Mind*, January 1933, pp. 50–52, and *Mind*, April 1933, pp. 191–5). But I believe that it is not ambiguous; I believe that its use is fixed by its context. Hence its use in a sentence does not make it impossible to know what is being expressed by that sentence.

(*b*) On the other hand, I admit that I have here provided no answer to the question, "What is the ultimate nature of facts?". But I have two excuses: (i) It is quite possible almost to complete philosophy without answering that question; (ii) Although some facts are such that one can give an account of their ultimate nature or structure, this can be done only in terms of other *atomic* facts. To state these atomic facts is to exhibit their structure, and the structure of atomic facts is identical with their ultimate structure. Hence when they are stated nothing more can be done. Even if they are reducible to events (see "Logical Constructions", *Mind*, October 1931, pp. 460–9) this reduction cannot be carried out by human beings; because sentences which *show* times are out of the question.

I do not attempt to define 'fact'. I describe[1] a fact as what a sentence expresses.

The student of language distinguishes between many different kinds of sentence. With many of these distinctions the philosopher is not concerned. The philosopher is concerned only with those distinctions among sentences which are associated with distinctions between the kinds of fact expressed by the sentence. Thus the philosopher is not concerned with a classification of sentences into French, German, etc. On the other hand, some distinctions among sentences are very important to the logician and even to the philosopher; because some distinctions among sentences *are* associated with distinctions among the kind of fact expressed. Further, some distinctions among the kinds of words which make up sentences are important to the philosopher, namely those which are associated with different functions among the elements of the fact expressed.

The first linguistic distinction important for the philosopher is that between complete and incomplete sentences. For the present we will ignore incomplete sentences and incomplete facts. Complete sentences are those which are made up of (*a*) proper names and demonstrative pronouns, and (*b*) adjectives, verbs and prepositions. Thus we have: (i) (*a*) This is *white*, (*b*) That is *black*; (ii) (*a*) Jack *loves* William, (*b*) Bob *loves* Bill; (iii) (*a*) Othello *prefers* Desdemona to Cassio, (*b*) Othello is *jealous* of Desdemona on account of Cassio.

Consider the pair of facts expressed by the first pair of

[1] I cannot *define* a fact as what a sentence expresses. For I define a sentence as what is intended to express a fact.

sentences. "It is clear", as Mr Mace says,[1] "that these two facts differ in two ways. They differ firstly in the way represented by the difference between 'this' and 'that'; and they differ, secondly, in the way represented by the phrases 'is white' and 'is black'. It is to be noted that we have here not only two differences, but two *kinds of difference*. The difference between these two kinds of difference may be expressed in various ways. We may say that the first kind of difference is merely that between the things we are speaking about, the second is a difference in what is being said about them. Again we may say that the terms *A* and *B*, 'this' and 'that', signify merely that the two things are 'numerically distinct' or 'other than' each other without implying any difference in character. The second kind of difference is a difference in character. In saying *A is white and C is white* we express otherness without difference in character. In saying *B is black and B is round* we express difference in character without otherness. The statement *A is white and B is black* combines both kinds of distinction.

"The matter has been expressed rather more technically in the following way. It may be supposed that the facts are in some way complex. It is therefore suggested (that in the case under consideration) each is constituted by the union of two elements, and that the elements are of two kinds which may be called respectively '*constituents*' and '*components*'. The constituents in a fact...are the elements in virtue of which one characterized thing might be merely numerically distinct from another, i.e. distinct without difference in character. The components

[1] *Principles of Logic*, p. 40.

of a fact are elements which can in a certain sense be 'shared' in common with things which are numerically distinct. If A is white and C is white, A is other than C, but whiteness is shared by both. It is their 'common property'.... These facts therefore (facts of the kind A is white, B is black, etc.) are constituted by the union of two elements, one constituent...and one component.... Components which require to be united only with one constituent to constitute a fact are called qualities.

"Some components require to be combined with more than one constituent in order to constitute a fact. Such components are called relations. Such a mode of union is illustrated by the fact *A is smaller than B*. For certain purposes, and in a certain sense, it is permissible to say that in this fact also we may distinguish two 'parts'— the [subject] represented by A and the [predicate] represented by the phrase 'is smaller than B'. But it is evident that such an analysis is not ultimate. 'Being smaller than B' is not so simple a character as 'being white'. [Indeed it is not strictly a character at all and if we were to call it the component of the fact we should be obliged to say that the component contained a constituent B.][1] A more ultimate account of the fact is given by saying that it is constituted by three elements, the [constituent] A, the [constituent] B and the relation 'is smaller than'.

"The relation expressed by 'is smaller than' is what is called a 'dyadic' relation. It requires two 'terms'.

[1] Square brackets indicate slight difference from Mr Mace's version.

There are, however, triadic, tetradic and more complex relations."

Difference in both constituent and component is illustrated in our first pair of examples. Difference in constituent without difference in component is illustrated in our second pair. Difference in component without difference in constituent is illustrated in our third pair. Our first pair of facts are monadic in form, our second dyadic, our third triadic.

These examples should cause you to see what is meant by 'constituent' and 'component' and 'form'. I cannot define these words. There are, however, three ways of picking out what I mean. (1) Each fact which is not made up of other facts has only one *component*. Its *component* is that one of its elements which fixes its form. Thus if a fact contains *adjoins* as *component* it must be dyadic. The *constituents* of a fact are those of its elements other than its components. (2) I cannot define 'fact' but it is not useless to write: A fact is the qualifying of something by a quality or the relating of something to one or more things by a relation.[1] To say that *C* is *component* in the fact *F* is to say that *C* qualifies or relates in *F*. To say that *C* is a *constituent* in the fact *F* is to say that *C* is qualified or related in *F*. The *elements* of *F* are its components and constituents. (3) If *F* can be expressed by the sentence 'a R b' or 'b R a' or 'd R b c' or 'b R d c' or 'b R c d', etc. then b is a constituent of *F*. Two facts have the same *form* when they have the same number of constituents. Two facts have a different *arrangement* when they have the same elements but these

[1] Cf. MacTaggart, *Nature of Existence*, p. 11.

elements have a different order in each, e.g. *She loves him* and *He loves her.* Two facts cannot have the same arrangement, for then they would have the same form and the same elements arranged in the same order so that there would not be two facts but one fact.

3.2. UNIVERSALS AND PARTICULARS. This is a difficult distinction. It is possible to understand fairly clearly the subsequent discussions in this book without considering it. On the other hand, when this distinction is seen the subsequent discussions will often be understood much more clearly. Universals are qualities and relations. Particulars are this's and that's. Universals or characters are named by adjectives, prepositions and verbs; particulars by demonstrative pronouns and proper names. If we described universals as the components of facts and particulars as the constituents of facts, we should not be far wrong. Nevertheless we should not be quite right. For universals are sometimes constituents in facts. Thus *orange, red* and *yellow* are constituents in *Orange is between red and yellow.* On the other hand particulars are never anything but constituents of facts. Hence we may amend our description of universals and particulars as follows: Universals can function in a fact either as components or constituents. Particulars can function only as constituents. It seems to me that this difference in function is dependent upon a difference in 'inner nature'. I cannot define this inner difference between universals and particulars, but I expect that if you set down examples of each you will see it. To speak of *this* and *that* without mentioning the universals which

25

characterize them is to speak with force but without colour, and therefore uninterestingly. To speak of *loving* and *hating* without mentioning whether they relate particulars or are merely unrealised possibilities is to speak with colour but without force, and therefore again uninterestingly. It is only fact which is interesting. For in the fact the universal colours the particular and the particular energises the universal.

But this metaphor does not express the inner difference. For what does the metaphor come to? Just this: Universals qualify and relate particulars and particulars give existence to universals. And this is where we started.[1]

There is in logic another use of the words 'particular' and 'universal' which must be mentioned in order to prevent confusion with that which we have just considered. This is a use in which the words are applicable to facts and propositions. Facts of the form *Everything which has the character S has the character P*, e.g. *Everything which is a Frenchman is a patriot*, are universal facts. Facts of the form *Something which has S has P*, e.g. *Some Frenchmen are patriots*, are particular facts.

It is now possible to say more exactly what I meant when I said that the scientist seeks *universal* causal facts. I was saying two things at once: (i) that the scientist seeks causal facts which are universal in the logician's sense of being about everything which has such and such a character; (ii) that the scientist seeks causal facts which are universal in the sense that they contain no particulars but only universals.

[1] See App. II.

The exact sense in which the facts of science do not contain particulars but only universals calls for a word of explanation. We have already noticed a fact which contains only universals, the fact *Orange is between red and yellow*. But this is a *complete* fact, and it contains only universals because all its elements, even its constituents, are universals. Now the facts of science contain only universals as elements, but they do so only by being *incomplete* and omitting the particular elements in complete facts. Incomplete facts are those facts which are expressed by incomplete sentences. Simple incomplete sentences are obtained from simple complete sentences by omitting one of the names which make them up and filling the gap in the sentence with the word 'something' or '*x*' or some other mark equally non-informative. Thus take the complete sentence "Wang is happy". Omit 'Wang' and write "Something is happy". The first sentence mentions a particular; the second does not, but saves itself from doing so only by becoming incomplete and expressing an incomplete fact. You can see why I say that the fact which "Something is happy" expresses is incomplete. There are two objections to saying that it is complete. (*a*) It is plain that there are not two facts (1) *Wang is happy*, and (2) *Something is happy*; *Something is happy* is not *another* fact in the way that *Wong is happy* would be. (*b*) If possible, let *Something is happy* be a complete fact. Then what are its elements? Not just the quality *happy*. Not Wang and *happy*; for then it would be identical with *Wang is happy*. And yet nothing other than Wang will fill the bill; Wong and Wing will not do. Nor will it do to say that *Something is happy* is the fact *It is not the case that Wang is not happy and Wong is not happy and Wing is not happy and etc.* For we can certainly know that something is happy without thinking of Wong and Wing and all the other things which might be happy[1] and then denying that each and all lack happiness. Finally it will not do to say that something which is neither one thing nor another, namely *something*, is the missing constituent; for that would be not mythology but nonsense. Therefore "Something is happy" does not express a complete fact. And as it is usual to say nevertheless that it expresses a fact, we are tempted to say that it expresses an incomplete fact. It would be better to say that it incompletely expresses an ordinary complete fact, namely in this case, *Wang is happy*. In general then: "The fact *Something has P* is an incomplete fact" means "The sentence 'Something has *P*' incompletely expresses a fact (complete)".

Now obviously the fact *Something is a Chinaman and the same thing is happy*, i.e. *Some Chinaman is happy* is incomplete in the same sense. And since the universal fact *Every Chinaman is happy* means *Something is a Chinaman and happy and it is not the case that something is a Chinaman and not happy* it also is incomplete in this sense.

We can now say what was meant by saying that the laws of science do not mention particulars though they apply to particulars. The laws of science are universal and therefore incomplete in the sense just indicated. The

[1] See Moore, *Facts and Propositions*, Aristotelian Society, Supplementary Vol. VII.

laws of science contain no particulars only because they are incomplete forms of complete facts which do contain particulars. This is better put by saying: The sentences of science incompletely express facts (complete). They name no particulars, but the facts which they incompletely express contain particulars. It must be remembered that, when we say that the sentences of science incompletely express facts (complete), we do *not* mean that they incompletely or imperfectly express the facts (incomplete) which they are intended to express.

It is thus clear that we can speak about incomplete facts only because there are complete facts and sentences which incompletely express them.

3.3. GENERIC AND SPECIFIC. Sometimes one universal *C'* *specifies* another, *C*, then *C'* is *more specific than C* and *C more generic than C'*. The meaning of 'specifies' is best pointed out by examples and the examples are conveniently given in diagrams. In the diagrams '*C → C'*' means "*C* is *specified* in *C'*", i.e. "*C' specifies C*".

It will be noticed that if *C* (e.g. coloured) is specified in *C'* (e.g. red) then (i) if a thing has *C'* (red) it must have *C* (coloured) because *C* (coloured) will be included in *C'* (red); (ii) if a thing has *C* (coloured) it must have *some* character like *C'* (red) which is a specific form of *C* (coloured) but this character need not of course be *C'* (red). From (i) it follows that (iii) to say of a thing that it has *C'* is to say more about it than to say that it has *C*. Thus if I say "Bob is running swiftly" I tell you more than if I say "Bob is running". On the other hand this something more cannot be separately stated. I cannot translate "Bob is running swiftly" into "Bob is running and Bob is swiftly"; for the second sentence, of course,

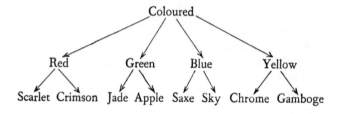

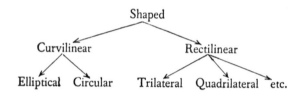

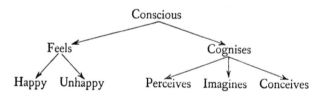

is nonsense. It follows that we cannot say that *red and hard* specifies *red*; although *red and hard* is related to *red* as stated in (i), (ii) and (iii). And *red* is not a specific form of *red or hard* though here again (i), (ii) and (iii) are satisfied. The fact is *red and hard* and *red or hard* are not universals; for strictly there are no conjunctive or disjunctive universals but only conjunctive and disjunctive facts. "This is red or hard" means "Either this is red or this is hard".

We can now improve three definitions which have been given above. (1) The scientist seeks generic facts in the sense that he seeks facts which are concerned with universals which are very generic. This is because such facts have a greater range.

(2) A mental fact is one which contains as component *conscious* or some universal which specifies *conscious*.

(3) A material fact is one which contains as component some species of *has a spatial character* or some species of *has some extensive character*, or some combination of these.

3.4. FACTS AND EVENTS. Consider a fact which is complete, particular, and absolutely specific. *This is R*, where '*R*' names an absolutely specific shade of red is such a fact; and *This P that*, where *P* stands for some absolutely specific form of pulling, i.e. pulling with such and such force, etc., is such a fact; and *Alfred is frightened in such and such a degree by Beatrice* is another complete, particular and specific fact.

Now every fact is in a sense instantaneous, it is concerned with one moment. Thus "That is red" means "That is red now", i.e. "That is red at this moment". Facts are *at* a time. This makes it impossible to *identify* a fact with an event; for an event *occupies* a period of time however short.

On the other hand, to every fact which is complete, particular and specific there corresponds an event including the same particular and the same universal and occupying a period which contains the moment which the fact is *at*. We may say that each complete, particular, and specific fact is an infinitely thin temporal slice of an event. Thus *This buzzes now* is a fact which is a slice out of a buzzing. *He is depressed now* is a slice out of the event which occupied perhaps the greater part of a week. *He is flat out now*[1] is a slice out of a gallop, which is an event. Roughly speaking, we may say that an event is a series of complete, particular, specific facts, just as a moving picture of a gallop which you see at the cinema is a series of pictures of the horse at a series of moments. Sometimes a series is uniform,[2] containing the same component throughout. Thus my depression may remain constant in quality and degree. Sometimes a series is non-uniform, i.e. the component varies from moment to moment. Thus my depression may increase perhaps steadily, perhaps unsteadily; and a race is a characteristic *pattern* of facts. It is important to notice that events and facts are built from the same materials and have a similar form; both have components and constituents. This will be kept in mind if we remember that an event is a pattern of complete, particular, specific

[1] Not in the usual sense of 'flat out', which means merely 'at full speed' and might be applied to a motor-cycle; but in a more literal sense referring to the horse's position at the gallop.

[2] A uniform series gives a state rather than an event. 'Event' strictly implies change.

facts and a complete, particular, specific fact is an in-finitely thin slice out of an event.[1]

4. **The Relations of Matter and Mind.**[2] Amongst the many relations between matter and mind there are two which we shall study in this book: first the relation of ownership, and second the relation of knowledge.

A mind is a cluster of mental facts which are all about the same thing.[3] A material thing is a cluster of material facts which are all facts about the same thing.

Each mind *owns* in a special sense one material thing, namely its body. And each mind knows by perception and in other ways a great many material things. It is with the analysis of these relations that we shall now concern ourselves.

FURTHER READING

Analytic and speculative philosophy: Broad, *Scientific Thought*, pp. 11–25.

Mental facts: Moore, *British Contemporary Philosophy*, vol. (ii), p. 209.

Generic and specific characters: W. E. Johnson, *Logic*, vol. (i), chap. XI.

[1] This is not the place to decide whether facts or events are the more fundamental. For further discussion see "Logical Constructions", *Mind*, October, 1931, pp. 461–9.

[2] Throughout this book 'mind' has the current philosophical use according to which it includes not merely the intellectual or cognitive part of a man's nature but also his feelings.

[3] The analysis of *the same thing* is one of the hardest in metaphysics.

PART I

Body and Mind

CHAPTER I

THE ANALYTIC PROBLEM ABOUT OWNERSHIP

It is usual to speak of "*the* problem of body and mind" or of "the problem of *the* relation between body and mind". This is a vague and unsatisfactory way of speaking. For there are millions of relations between bodies and minds, and how are we to know from such a vague description which relation it is with which we are to concern ourselves? (The first precept for philosophic analysing is this: Know clearly what it is you propose to analyse.[1]) We must, therefore, make an attempt to describe more exactly the kind of fact we wish to analyse. This can be done as follows: I call a certain body mine, you call a certain other body yours, and Bob calls a certain other body his. Let us name the relation which everybody speaks of in this way by calling a certain body his own, the relation of *ownership*. This, I think, is the relation of which those who speak about *the* relation between body and mind are thinking. Although I have called the relation 'ownership' because it is expressed by the use of the possessive pronoun it is clear nevertheless that a man does not own his body in the same sense as that in which he owns his pen. We may say if we like

[1] We can know clearly without knowing the analysis. You can see a house clearly without knowing its structure. And you can know what, for example, 'true' means without knowing its formal definition.

that the sense in which he owns his body is 'more intimate'. Our problem is: What is ownership in this intimate sense? [*More accurately*: What is the relation between a mind and a body which is involved in the fact that they are both owned by the same person?][1]

This question we cannot hope to answer in this small book. All we shall do is to consider what, if any, part in the analysis of ownership is played by the causal rela-

---

[1] It is important to notice the amendment in brackets, for I now find a serious confusion in the text. It is too late to remove it. Besides, it provides an instructive example of bad philosophising. The reader will not be misled if it is pointed out here.

I write in the text as if the relation between mind and body is the same as the relation between man and body. In other words, I write as if the relation between John Brown and his body is the same as the relation between John Brown's mind and his body. Thus I tacitly identify John Brown with his mind or soul.

Even if such identification were in some sense correct it is most improper to write at this stage in such a way as to presuppose its correctness.

What I ought to have written was this: We all know the relation of ownership between John Brown and a certain body which we refer to by calling that body his. And we all know that relation of ownership between John Brown and a certain mind which we refer to by calling that mind his. And now we can all see a relation between John Brown's mind and John Brown's body which holds in virtue of the fact that they are a body and mind *owned by the same person*. That relation is the one called *the* relation between body and mind. Consequently when subsequently I write of the relation between body and mind it must be remembered that it is not the relation of ownership which holds between a person and his body but a relation which is intimately related to that ownership in the way indicated in this paragraph.

tion. It seems clear that my mind affects in greater degree and more directly my body than it does anyone else's body, and that the events in my mind are partly and perhaps wholly due to events in my body. Is this what I *mean* by calling my body mine? The answer to this philosophical question about the analysis of ownership depends partly upon the answer we give to three questions of fact concerning the causal relations, if any, between bodily and mental events. These questions are:

I. Is there *any* kind of causal relation between bodily and mental events?

II. Do bodily events ever *form part of the cause* of mental events and vice versa?

III. Do bodily events ever *form the whole cause* of mental events and vice versa?

But before considering even these preliminary questions we must (*a*) make quite sure that we see clearly the distinction between bodily and mental events, and (*b*) set down the known correlations, as opposed to causal relations, between the two.

CHAPTER II

DISTINCTION BETWEEN MENTAL AND NERVOUS EVENTS

It is usually supposed that the mental events most directly due to bodily events are sensations, while the mental events to which bodily events are most directly due are decisions. A pin pricks my skin and I then have a sensation of pain; I decide to swing my arm and it then begins to swing. The bodily events most closely connected with the mental events are certain changes in the nerves of my body. The piercing of my skin is followed by a sensation of pain, but not at once; between the piercing and the pain a change passes up a nerve running from the skin to the mass of nerve cells which is my brain. And my decision to move my arm is followed by the movement, but not at once; between the decision and the movement a short but measurable time elapses, and during this time a change is travelling down a nerve from my brain to the muscle of my arm. The material and mental events which are most likely to be confused are these closely connected events, sensations and decisions on the one hand, and nervous changes on the other. Let us consider the nature of these events in rather greater detail with a view to removing the remotest possibility of confusion. Then we may consider the established facts about the correlation between nervous events and sensations and decisions, with a view to deciding whether these correlations indicate a causa connexion.

1. **Sensations and Decisions.** It is not important for our purpose that we should find very exact definitions of sensations and decisions.

1.1. DECISIONS present no difficulty. Everyone knows what "I decided to blow up the train" means. Clearly the sentence expresses a mental fact in our sense. It implies that I foresaw a certain situation, namely the blowing up of the train; it implies the belief that I could produce that situation; and it implies something further, something characteristic of decision, a "giving of my-self" to the production of that situation. It does not, by the way, imply that I desire the situation for its own sake; I may be very averse to the blowing up of a train, es-pecially with passengers in it, and yet decide to blow it up in order to provide pleasure for the public.

1.2. SENSATIONS are rather more difficult. The word is usually understandable in its ordinary contexts. But here the context will be unfamiliar and a word of ex-planation is necessary. The following sentences express facts which are sensations, "I see this brown patch", "I hear that high note", "I feel a cool patch". These facts could also be expressed by, "I sense this as brown", "I sense that as high-pitched", "I sense something cool". We could add, of course, "I sense something musty", "I sense something bitter". All these facts are due to contact between some part of the external surface of the body and its environment. We must add organic sensations, headaches, stomachaches. And finally we must add after-sensations. You may obtain an after-sensation by looking at a piece of red paper on a grey background for twenty seconds and then, without shifting your eyes from the background, removing the red paper, leaving only the grey background. You will see a green patch. Again, if you gaze at an electric light for thirty seconds and then switch it off and gaze into the darkness, you will get an amusing series of after-sensations. After-sensations do not seem to reveal the nature of some material thing in the way other sensations do.

I can define what I am going to mean by a 'sensation' as follows: A sensation occurs when and only when someone *senses* something *as having* a certain *sense-quality*. Thus a sensation is a fact containing as constituents two particulars and a sense-quality, and as component the relation *senses-as-having*. One particular is always a person, the other is that which the person senses as having the sense-quality. I have not defined *senses-as-having* nor *sense-quality*; I cannot. *Senses-as-having* is the relation specified in *seeing*, *hearing* and *smelling*, as applied, not to *things*, such as chairs and trees, but as applied to patches and sounds. *Has a sense quality* is specified in *red*, *high-pitched*, *musty*, *bitter*. It is true, I think, of every sense-quality that it is extensive.

2. **The Nervous System.** Before considering the nature of nervous events, it will be well to describe briefly the nervous system.

2.1. DEFINITION. "The animal body is built up of

living cells of varying form and function."[1] Some of these cells form themselves into organs (such as the eye) which are peculiarly susceptible to certain changes in the environment—the eye to light-vibrations in the aether, the ear to sound-vibrations in the atmosphere.[2] Such organs are called 'receptors'. And some of the cells form themselves into organs which are specially important in the production of those changes in the condition of the body by which it adapts itself to its environment. Such organs are called 'effectors'. Muscles, glands and blood vessels are effectors. The contracting and relaxing of muscles and blood vessels and the secreting of glands are adaptations or *vital reactions*.

The *nervous system* is that network of cells, within the mass of cells making up a body, which connects the receptors of that body with its effectors. It connects them in the sense that the cells form nervous tissue which joins the receptors to the effectors, and in the sense that stimulation of the receptors sets up a train of changes in the nervous tissue joining them to the effectors, which brings about characteristic change (appropriate reaction) in the effectors. Nervous tissue then is the tissue which communicates environmental disturbance from the receptors to the effectors. Given such and such an environmental disturbance, there will be such and such an

[1] Collins and Drever, *Experimental Psychology*, p. 275. An excellent and fuller, though still compressed, account of the nervous system will be found in this book.

[2] Here and later in this account of the nervous system I am indebted to Mr H. H. Ferguson.

effect in the effectors. The nature of this effect cannot be predicted, at present at least, by the laws of mechanics. Special laws governing living bodies, and in more complicated cases where the mind interferes, laws about minds, are required for the prediction of a body's response to a given stimulus. That is why these responses are called *vital* reactions, as opposed to mechanical or chemical reactions.

2.2. STRUCTURE. Nervous tissue is made up of neurons. The neuron is the structural unit of the nervous system. It consists of a cell body and one or more outgrowths. There are two kinds of outgrowth. One kind receives the nervous impulse and transmits it *to* the cell body. These are the *dendrites*. As a rule they grow from the cell body as thick stems which soon break up into a number of fine filaments. The other kind transmits impulses outwards *from* the cell body. These are *axons*. Only one axon leaves each cell body. It is usually long and gives off branches at intervals (collaterals). Each of these and the main stem break up finally into fine filaments.

Each neuron links up with others in that the filaments at the ends of the one intertwine with, without being joined to, the filaments at the ends of others—axon filaments with dendron filaments and vice versa. Such an intertwining of filaments is called a *synapse*. A nervous impulse passes from one neuron to another as an electric current passes from one set of wires to another when they are intertwined.

A series of neurons linked together in this way form

a circuit which runs from a receptor to the spinal cord or brain and thence to an effector. These circuits are called *nervous arcs*. Each nervous arc contains: (i) an afferent[1] neuron or neurons which conveys an impulse towards the brain or spinal cord; (ii) connector neurons which convey the impulse from the afferent neuron to the efferent neuron; (iii) an efferent neuron or neurons, which conveys the impulse to some muscle or gland.

The synapse is supposed to offer more or less resistance to the passage of an impulse. Each receptor is connected with every effector by some route; and it is only the great resistance at some synapses which prevents an impulse from spreading all over the nervous system and makes it take one route rather than another out of the millions open to it.

Nerves are made of bundles of nerve fibres. Afferent nerves convey impulses towards the spinal cord and brain from the receptors, and efferent nerves convey impulses from the spinal cord and brain to the effectors. *Ganglia* are groups of nerve cells.

The nervous system has three main parts: (i) the central system; (ii) the peripheral system; (iii) the autonomic system.

(i) The central nervous system is composed of the sensory ganglia, the spinal cord and the brain. It consists largely of cell bodies.

(ii) The peripheral nervous system is composed of

---

[1] An afferent neuron must be distinguished from a dendron and an efferent neuron from an axon. An afferent neuron will have its axon nearer the brain than its dendron; the opposite holds of the efferent neuron.

those afferent and efferent nerves which convey impulses from the receptors to the central nervous system and thence to the effectors.

(iii) The autonomic system controls the activity of the involuntary muscles, e.g. those of the stomach and glands. It is partly controlled by the spinal cord and brain and partly by the secretions of the glands.

The central nervous system becomes more and more complicated as it passes up inside the vertebral column to the skull. The peripheral spinal nerves enter and pass out from the spinal cord through spaces between the vertebrae. The main parts of the brain are the medulla, the cerebellum, the pons, the basal ganglia and the cerebral hemispheres. Part of the cerebral hemispheres is made of cell bodies. This is the cortex. The cortex is a thin sheet of grey matter which lies above and around the basal ganglia, almost completely surrounding them. The surface of the cortex is convoluted.

The central nervous system is like a metropolis; in it there are many centres, through it there are many routes, and into it and out of it run many one-way routes (afferent and efferent nerves) from the provinces (receptors and effectors).

2.3. THE FUNCTIONING OF THE NERVOUS SYSTEM. The functioning of the nervous system involves five successive steps: (i) stimulation of a receptor, (ii) conduction of an impulse towards the central nervous system, (iii) adjustment of impulses within the central nervous system, (iv) conduction of an impulse from the central nervous system to an effector, (v) response of an effector.

Such a description covers processes of very different complexity. The impulse may travel a long and complicated route through the central nervous system and pass up to and then down from the higher centres in the brain. This happens when there is sensation and voluntary response. On the other hand the impulse may take a short route through the central nervous system; it may pass into and out of the spinal cord without visiting the brain. This happens in the case of the spinal reflex. Even after the brain of a frog has been removed, when acid is applied to its side it will scratch with its leg. This reaction depends upon a reflex arc consisting of afferent neurons, central neurons *within the spine*, and efferent neurons.

3. **Nervous Events.** It has been discovered that whenever anyone sees something as brown or hears something as squeaky, in the sense explained, then that seeing and hearing has followed upon a bodily disturbance. Take the case of hearing. When you say "I hear a noise", then a very short but measurable time before you hear the noise there is a disturbance of a special kind in your ear. Small particles of the atmosphere strike repeatedly upon your ear drum causing it to vibrate. Your ear drum is connected by a chain of three small bones to a membrane covering one end of a spiral tube in the inner ear. Consequently a vibration of your ear drum is transmitted through the chain of bones to the small membrane at the end of the tube. This tube is closed at the other end and is filled with a liquid, the perilymph. Consequently vibration in the small membrane attached to the three bones causes vibration, in

the form of a wave, to pass through the perilymph. Within the first tube is another, the walls of which are partly membranous and it is filled with endolymph. Consequently vibrations in the perilymph cause vibrations in the membranous wall of the inner tube and waves in the endolymph. Growing from the membranous walls and sticking into the endolymph are small hairs. The vibrations in the endolymph cause these hairs to vibrate. Joined to the roots of these hairs is the auditory nerve. The vibration of the hairs causes an invisible change to pass periodically up the auditory nerve to a special piece of the grey stuff in the brain, called the auditory centre. It is called the auditory centre because the invisible changes produced in it by the changes in the auditory nerve are always followed by the hearing of a sound.

This invisible change in the auditory nerve and nerve centres is called a nervous impulse. What is the nature of this change? The nature of the changes in the ear is plain enough. They consist of small movements in the ear drum, the small bones, the perilymph, etc., and each successive movement produces the next in accordance with the simple laws of mechanics. What about the change in the nerve? No visible vibration can be detected even with the most powerful microscopes. No doubt ultimately (in the scientist's sense) it consists in movements among the atoms which make up the nerve. But the change cannot be said to be a *perceptible* movement or mechanical change, in the sense in which this can be said of the disturbance in the ear. Indeed there is no perceptible change in the nerve. We know that there must be a change which passes up the nerve because when the nerve is intact and a certain event, e.g. the movement of hair cells, takes place at one end, another event takes place, namely a sensation; while, if the nerve is severed at any point, this sensation does not take place. No perceptible change takes place in the nerve and yet some change takes place. It is annoying that this change cannot be observed, but there is no need to become mysterious about it, much less to say that the nerves think or feel.[1] There are plenty of other cases in which we know that there is some change taking place in a material thing when we are unable to observe that change—for example, this is so when an electric current passes along a wire. In these other cases we do not hurry to suppose that a spirit is present in the wire and that it is his agency which insures that when a certain kind of event occurs at one end there will always follow a certain kind of event at the other. It is more plausible to suppose that the wire contains invisible and extremely minute particles and that the physical laws which hold of big, perceptible things hold of these also. In this way when a change in a wire is unobservable, so that we cannot observe its internal nature,[2] but only its effects, we are sometimes able to make a guess about the internal nature of the change and to say, for example, that it consists in such and such a redistribution of the atoms making up the wire. The more we know of the causal properties, that is the effects, of an imperceptible change,

[1] That is why it is dangerous to say that the nerves "pass messages along". It suggests that they decide to pass messages.
[2] The internal nature of an event are those qualities and relations which are components in the event.

49

the more likely we are to guess rightly about its internal nature and about the laws according to which its successive phases follow one another. We may ask whether a nervous event is the sort of microscopic change the phases of which succeed one another according to physical laws. Or is it the sort of microscopic change the phases of which succeed one another according to chemical laws? Or is it the sort of microscopic change the phases of which succeed one another according to laws peculiar to microscopic particles which make up living things? But these questions concerning the laws which govern the succession of the phases of a nervous event are irrelevant to our question. For we are concerned, not with these laws, but with the internal nature of the phases—the kind of qualities and relations manifested in them. And, whatever the laws, there is no doubt that this internal nature is material.

There is really no need for us to go further. The passage of a nervous impulse is a material process; it consists probably in a succession of bumps and bangs; these are all material events though they happen to be so small as to be unobservable even under high-powered microscopes. There is no need for us to bother about the specific nature of these bumps and bangs, nor about the laws which govern their succession. As to the laws, it may be added as a matter of interest that

Sir Charles Sherrington's long and brilliant work on brain and nerves has led to a constant increase in the discovery of functions that are due to mechanism....In two...discourses delivered at the Royal Institution and subsequently summarized in *Nature*, Professor E. D. Adrian has described recent advances in knowledge tending to show that the conduction of nervous impulses is a definite physical phenomenon.

A very close model of the nerve fibres along which messages travel is provided by an iron wire immersed in strong nitric acid, its surface thus becoming coated with a layer of 'passive' iron which prevents the acid from acting any further. If the film of passive iron is destroyed at any point, the difference of potential between the active and passive iron produces an electric current which has the effect of destroying the passive iron in the next section of the wire, and at the same time of restoring it where it was first destroyed. The area of surface change spreads down the wire accompanied by an electric change which is a close copy of the action current in a nerve. When the impulse passes down the nerve fibre, there appears to be a definite series of changes following one another with mechanical regularity, changes which can be made to recur again and again, yielding similar measurements whenever there are instruments sensitive enough to record them.

By the use of the triode valve amplifier the smallest possible electric changes can not only be detected but even demonstrated on a loud speaker. In the case of sensory impulses, the stimulus can be arranged so as to affect only a single end-organ and, therefore, a single nerve fibre. The impulses are shown to have a frequency varying from five to 150 a second, and there is already some reason to suppose that the impulses from different sense organs are not exactly alike. Each impulse is a discrete change with definite time relations; there is no continuous activity, but between each impulse there must be a time for recovery, just as a gun has to be re-loaded before it can be fired again. Within the body, at least, brain messages to or fro travel only by a definite mechanism, comparable in every way with phenomena recognized as purely physico-chemical.[1]

[1] *The Times.*

4. **Confusion of Sensation with Stimulation.** There should now, I think, be no danger of confusing a sensation, as we have defined it, with the stimulation of the sense organ and nerve which precedes it. It should be clear that stimulation is a material event and sensation a mental event.

It is sometimes said that, though sensation involves consciousness and is thus a mental event, it is also a material event. This mistake is due to one or both of two confusions. (*a*) The word 'sensation' is sometimes used in such a way that a sensation is a psycho-physiological event including both (i) a stimulation of end-organ, nerve and brain, and (ii) the associated mental event which we have called "sensing something as having a sense-quality". If 'sensation' is used in this way then, of course, a sensation is both mental and material in the sense that it is a compound event containing both a material event and a mental event. (*b*) Every sensation contains an extensive quality as a *constituent*. But its component, the relation which unites its constituents into a unity, is not a space-relation nor an extensive quality. And we, superior in our exact definition of a material event (see p. 31), are able to see quite clearly that a sensation, as defined by us, is not a material event, however many extensive qualities it may contain as constituents.

CHAPTER III

DENIAL OF MENTAL EVENTS — MATERIALISM

There are people who have used language suggesting that they hold that there are no mental events but only bodily events. Do they mean (*a*) that whenever I speak about a mind, or thinking, or feeling, or wishing, or believing, then I speak falsely because it is never true that anyone thinks or feels? Or do they mean (*b*) that, though when I say "I am conscious" I speak truly and express a fact, it will be found on careful consideration that that fact consists ultimately of bodily and material facts. Both these doctrines are forms of materialism. We may call the first simple or pure[1] materialism.

1. **Simple Materialism.** Does the simple materialist believe that simple materialism is true? If so it is false. For then something is believing something. And according to simple materialism it is never true that something is thinking, feeling or believing. Again, I believe that simple materialism is false. Therefore it is false. For simple materialism implies that no one believes anything.

It may be objected that these arguments are frivolous, sophistical, and, in particular, question-begging. Does this mean (α) that among the premisses of my arguments I have surreptitiously included the conclusion I wish to

[1] Broad, *The Mind and Its Place in Nature*, p. 610.

prove, namely the contradictory of materialism? If so, I deny the accusation. To begin with materialism cannot be said to *be* the proposition *No one believes anything*. It will then be objected that materialism *contains* the proposition *No one believes anything* and that my argument is circular because it contains as a fundamental premiss the contradictory of what materialism contains.

But in the first place I should not allow that the sense of 'contains' in which materialism contains *No one believes anything* is a sense which would render my argument circular even if it contained *Someone believes something* as a fundamental premiss. And in the second place it is not the general or incomplete proposition *Someone believes something* which is my fundamental premiss but an instance of it, namely *This thing (I) believes this thing (that simple materialism is false)*. In a word my argument against materialism consists in testing it by applying it to particular cases.

"But", it may be said, "this distinction between general statement and particular case is trivial; you have practically included your conclusion among your premisses."

But 'trivial' means 'trivial for a certain purpose'. The distinction between the general statement and the particular case is trivial for some purposes. But it is not trivial for the purpose of ascertaining the truth of general and abstract philosophical doctrines. For, as Hume says, "It is easy for a false hypothesis to maintain some appearance of truth while it keeps wholly in generals".[1] We may indeed set down as a second philosophic pre-

[1] *The Principles of Morals*, App. 1.

cept: *To ascertain the truth of a general statement apply it in all sorts of particular instances.* Tested by this precept, simple materialism is clearly false.

(β) People sometimes call an argument question-begging when it includes a premiss which must be false if the view against which the argument is directed is true. Thus my argument against simple materialism includes the premiss *I believe, etc.*; and such a premiss must be false if simple materialism is true.

This criticism is muddle-headed. It would apply to any demonstrative refutation; for such a refutation is always of the form *P (premiss) entails the falsity of Q (view in question). P is true, therefore Q is false.* And if *P* entails that *Q* is false, then *Q* is true will entail that *P* is false. Hence if my argument against simple materialism does not involve a logical fallacy it will be open to this 'criticism'.[1]

(γ) It might be claimed that no materialist would admit my premiss. But even if this were true, it would have no tendency to show that my argument is unsound; at the most it would show that my argument is useless for converting confirmed simple materialists. If there are such people and they deny that they believe their own view, then there is nothing more to be said.

[1] Of course if *P* is less certain than *Q*, apart from the argument under consideration, then the argument is *useless*. All that a demonstrative argument does is to show that *P* and *Q* cannot both be true. A decision as to *which* is true can be reached only by considering their relative certainties *independently of the argument*. A person who argues *P, therefore Q is false, assumes* that *P* is the more certain.

But there are no confirmed simple materialists. For simple materialism has been held only by people who confuse it with analytic[1] materialism and even epiphenomenalism.

2. **Analytic Materialism.** This is the doctrine that, though when I say "I wish I were so and so" I express a fact, it will be found on careful consideration that that fact consists ultimately of material facts. It is the doctrine that "I believe that Bob is well" just means the same as some statement about my bodily condition, e.g. that my throat is uttering the words "Bob is well". In general then: Analytic materialism is the doctrine that mental facts are not an ultimately new kind of fact but a certain kind of complex of material facts.

The only kind of material fact to which it is plausible to reduce mental facts about X are facts about X's body. Hence analytic materialism becomes behaviourism. There are two kinds of analytic behaviourism. According to the first kind, when one says that such and such a mental state is occurring, one is just saying that a bodily state having such and such *internal characters* is occurring. According to the second kind, one is just saying that a bodily state which has such and such *causal properties* is occurring. Thus suppose it is held that "I believe that monkeys detest jaguars" means "This throat is uttering the words 'Monkeys detest jaguars'", such a view is an example of the first kind of materialism. Suppose, on the other hand, that some more subtle form

---

[1] What Broad calls reductive materialism (*The Mind and Its Place in Nature*, p. 610).

of behaviourism is adopted, according to which "I believe monkeys detest jaguars" means "This body is in a state which is liable to result in that group of reactions which is associated with confident utterance of 'Monkeys detest jaguars', namely keeping 'favourite' monkeys from jaguars and in general acting *as if* monkeys detested jaguars".

According to the first kind of analytic behaviourism, the bodily state to which the belief is reduced is defined as such and such a piece of behaviour. According to the second kind of behaviourism, the bodily state to which the belief is reduced is defined as the state which would, in response to stimulus S_1, produce behaviour R_1, and, in response to S_2, produce behaviour R_2, etc.

Dr Broad urges an objection which is fatal to both these views. He writes:

However completely the behaviour of an external body answers to the behaviouristic tests for intelligence it always remains a perfectly sensible question to ask; "Has it really got a mind or is it merely an automaton?" It is quite true that we have no available means of answering such questions conclusively. It is also true that the more nearly a body answers to the behaviouristic tests for intelligence, the harder it is for us in practice to contemplate the possibility of its having no mind. Still the question "Has it a mind?" is never silly in the sense that it is meaningless. At worst it is silly only in the sense that it does not generally express a real doubt, and that we have no means of answering it. It may be like asking whether the moon may not be made of green cheese; but it is not like asking whether a rich man may have no wealth. Now on the behaviouristic theory to have a mind means just to behave in certain ways, and to ask whether a thing which admittedly does behave in these ways has a mind would be like asking whether Jones who is admittedly a rich man, has much wealth. Since the question can be raised, and is evidently not tautologous or self-contradictory, it is clear that when we ascribe a mind or a mental process to an external body we do not mean simply that it behaves in certain characteristic ways.[1]

If the behaviourist answers that whatever we *do* mean this is all that we *ought* to mean he has returned to simple materialism, for he is denying that the beliefs that we do express by our psychological sentences, such as "I believe in materialism", are true.

We conclude, therefore, that (*a*) there are mental facts, and (*b*) these mental facts are not reducible to material facts.

We have not refuted the milder form of materialism called 'epiphenomenalism'. This is one of the views to which the question of the causal connexion of body and mind is relevant.

[1] Broad, *The Mind and Its Place in Nature*, p. 614. This is a common and important form of philosophical 'argument'. Instead of 'argument' perhaps one should say 'method of putting a question'. This would avoid the charge of circularity.

CHAPTER IV

CORRELATIONS BETWEEN BODILY AND MENTAL EVENTS

If there are two things such that whenever the one occurs the other occurs also, those two things are said to be 'associated'. Thus thunder is associated with lightning. And if there are two things such that any change in the one is accompanied by a change in the other, those two things are said to be, not merely associated, but 'correlated'. The heat of the weather is correlated with the height of the mercury in the thermometer. We will use 'correlation' in a broad sense both for strict correlation and association.

Correlation is usually, but not always, due to causal connexion. When S is correlated with B there is usually a causal connexion between them—either they are joint effects of a common cause, as with thunder and lightning, or the one is the effect of the other, as with speed and wind resistance, or draughts and colds. But there might be and sometimes is correlation without causal connexion. There was found to be a high correlation between the importation of bananas and marriages celebrated in the Church of England, but it is unlikely that there was any causal connexion here—it was a matter of chance. Again, suppose that every time you went for a picnic it rained. That would probably be correlation without causal connexion—unless indeed you selected rainy days.

Nevertheless correlation is an excellent sign of causal connexion, because almost always when there is prolonged correlation there is causal connexion. It is therefore important to set down the correlations between bodily and mental events if we are to decide whether there is causal connexion.

1. **Correlation of Development.** Only material things with nervous systems have minds. Further, the more complicated the nervous system, the more complicated the mind. This is easily seen in any diagram of the development of the brain from fish to man.

2. **Localization of Function.** Certain parts of the nervous system are associated with certain functions and other parts with other functions. Thus in the spinal cord are centres associated with spinal reflexes. This is proved by a well-known experiment.[1] James writes:

If, then, we reduce the frog's nervous system to the spinal cord alone, by making a section behind the base of the skull, between the spinal cord and the medulla oblongata, thereby cutting off the brain from all connection with the rest of the body, the frog will still continue to live, but with a very peculiarly modified activity. It ceases to breathe or swallow....If thrown on its back it lies there quietly without turning over like a normal frog. Locomotion and voice are abolished. [But] *if we suspend it by the nose and irritate different portions of its skin by acid, it performs a remarkable series of 'defensive' movements calculated to wipe away the irritant.*[2]

[1] Of course there is much else in the spinal cord—for example, fibres running down from the brain.

[2] William James, *Textbook of Psychology*, p. 92. Italics mine.

With the medulla restored the frog swallows. With the medulla and cerebellum together the frog jumps, swims and turns over from his back. A frog which lacks only the cerebral hemispheres differs from a normal frog only in that he undertakes no movements spontaneously. He does not go in search of insects, fish or smaller frogs.

It is clear that the different movements of the frog are produced by the same muscles. It is also clear that in the case of the less complicated movements the muscles are operated by less complicated parts of the nervous system, while in the case of the more complicated movements the muscles are operated by more complicated parts of the nervous system. This strongly suggests that the complicated voluntary movements of the higher animals and man are due to the action of the most complicated part of the nervous system, the cortex.

More information about the localization of function is obtained by other physiological methods. The results of electrical stimulation of different parts, mainly in the cerebral cortex, have been carefully observed. Again severed nerves degenerate and their course through the nervous system can then be traced. "Again, by correlating abnormal behaviour or functioning with pathological conditions in definite localities in the nervous centres, further light is thrown on the localization of functions."[1]

Finally, in the development of the brain from fish to man the brain grows larger and this increase in size is due almost wholly to the increase in size of a particular part of the brain, namely the cerebral

[1] Collins and Drever, *Experimental Psychology*, p. 295.

hemispheres. Now it is in voluntary movements that human functioning differs most from that of other animals. This suggests, of course, that the voluntary movements are dependent upon the cerebral hemispheres. And research has even established that certain voluntary movements and certain sensations are associated with certain parts of the hemispheres, and other movements and sensations with other parts. For example, visual sensations are associated with the occipital lobes. Now the voluntary movements are accompanied by mental events and sensations too are mental events.

3. Correlation with Disposition. An inefficient liver is associated with depression and irritability. Insufficient secretion from the thyroid gland is associated with the blunting of mental activities. Kretschmer[1] has established an association between the *pyknic* type of individual (roughly the short and broad type) and liability to manic-depressive mental disorder, and an association between the long-narrow type of individual and the mental disorder called *schizophrenia*. The more these facts are studied, the closer does the connexion appear to be.

4. Correlation of State with State. Finally we reach facts which suggest, perhaps even more strongly than the facts we have just considered, a causal connexion between body and mind. The facts under this head are well known to all of us, and their presence "at the back of our minds" explains our astonishment at the suggestion that body and mind do not interact. I shall

[1] *Physique and Character.*

claim that this astonishment is very rational. But first as to the facts.

4.1. CORRELATIONS SUGGESTING THE ACTION OF BODY ON MIND.

4.11. *Drugs.* Some drugs, such as alcohol, are associated with happiness. Others, such as chloroform, depress consciousness. Different amounts of drugs are associated with different degrees of happiness and consciousness; a sufficient amount is associated with death. In death, I assume, consciousness either ceases or goes on in a very different way.

4.12. *Stimulation and Sensation.* We have already seen that stimulation of one organ (the ear, say) is associated with one mode of sensation (hearing), while stimulation of another organ (the eye, say) is associated with another mode of sensation (seeing). But the co-variation of sensation with stimulation is more refined than this. Intensity of sensation (e.g. loudness of sound) varies with intensity of stimulus (e.g. amplitude of wave in the atmosphere). Quality of sensation (e.g. pitch of sound) varies with the frequency of the stimulus (e.g. frequency of wave in the atmosphere).[1]

4.2. CORRELATIONS SUGGESTING THE ACTION OF MIND ON BODY.

---

[1] A train of waves has great amplitude when the crests of the waves are high and the troughs are deep. It has high frequency when the distance between two adjacent crests or adjacent troughs is small.

4.21. *Voluntary movements.* Whenever I decide to make such and such a movement I make it unless I am suddenly paralysed or forcibly constrained from outside. Whenever I desire to swing my arm I swing it. And the co-variation of movement with decision is more refined than this. For the direction and intensity of the movement which I decide to carry out fixes the direction and intensity of the movement which I do carry out.

4.22. *Suggestion.* By the use of hypnotic suggestion, one of two exactly similar blisters has been made to heal distinctly more rapidly than the other. This is an example from among the many cases now known of the effect of suggestion upon the bodily condition.[1]

[1] McDougall, *Abnormal Psychology*, p. 101.

CHAPTER V

DO BODILY EVENTS OCCASION MENTAL EVENTS AND VICE VERSA?

1. **The Three Questions.** We must now discuss what causal relationship, if any, the correlations establish, and the view that in spite of the correlations there is no causal relationship. We want to know the answer to the following questions:

I. Is there *any* causal connexion between bodily and mental events?

II. Are bodily events ever *the occasion or part of the occasion* of mental events and vice versa?

III. Do bodily events ever *produce* mental events and vice versa?

2. **Question I. Causal Connexion.**

2.1. MEANING OF 'CAUSAL CONNEXION'. Two events may be causally connected either lineally or as effects of a common cause. Of two events which are lineally causally connected, one will be either directly or indirectly the cause of the other. Thus, when in shunting a bump is transmitted along a line of railway trucks, each earlier bump is lineally causally connected with each later bump. Of course only the penultimate bump is *directly* lineally causally connected with the ultimate bump.

There is sometimes non-lineal causal connexion

between two events; in which case one is neither directly nor indirectly the cause of the other. Thus thunder has a causal connexion with lightning; yet one is not the cause of the other, even indirectly; they are joint effects of a third event, an electrical disturbance.

2.2. EXISTENCE OF CAUSAL CONNEXION. The correlations between mind and body are perfect and refined. Whenever my retina is stimulated by light a sensation of a coloured patch follows. And the intensity and hue of the sensation vary with the intensity and frequency of the stimulation respectively. Such correlation as this would be counted, in any other department of science, excellent evidence for causal connexion of some sort. Hence we conclude that either (α) bodily events are the causes of mental events, or (β) they are joint effects of some third kind of event. (I should require good reason for rejecting (α) before accepting (β) with its mysterious third unobserved kind of event.)

3. Question II. Occasioning.

3.1. MEANING OF 'OCCASION'. In order to see the difference between question II, "Do bodily events *occasion* mental events?" and question III, "Do bodily events *completely explain* mental events?" we must see the difference between what *occasions* an event and what *completely explains* an event. Consider the series of bumps which passes along a line of railway trucks. We might say that the cause of the movement of the last truck was the movement of the last but one. Someone might object to this statement and say that the movement of the first truck was part of the cause of the movement of the last. This objection is trivial because we meant that the *direct* cause of the movement of the last truck was the movement of the last but one. This statement, however, is still open to a rather more serious objection. For clearly the movement of the penultimate truck would not have caused the movement of the ultimate truck if the ultimate truck had not been next to it. Hence the change in position of the penultimate truck does not provide the complete explanation of the movement of the ultimate truck. The previous condition of the penultimate truck, its proximity to the ultimate truck, forms part of the complete explanation of the movement of the ultimate truck. The complete explanation of an event or change E_2 involves usually both (i) a previous change, E_1, and (ii) the presence of certain other circumstances which remain unchanged. Let us call the previous change the *occasion* of E_2, and the other circumstances which are also necessary to the occurrence of E_2 the *conditions* of E_2. Thus the occasion of a sensation may be a disturbance in the brain, although such a disturbance might have been ineffective if the brain had not been 'furnished' with a mind.

3.2. ARGUMENTS FOR OCCASIONING.

3.21. I believe that bodily events occasion, or at least form part of the occasion of mental events. I justify this belief as follows:

(i) *Inspection.* I believe that, when I watch myself stick a pin in my finger, I know then without argument that that pin-sticking occasioned the pain.[1] It may be objected that I do not know this without argument, although the argument has become unconscious; that I really rely upon the correlation between the pricking and the pain. Against this suggestion there are two objections: In the first place it must be remembered that many people do not know many of those correlations between the disturbance in an end-organ and the sensation which follows which were set out in the last chapter. Yet they are as certain as I am that the pin occasions their pain. In the second place, there is an obvious difference between inferring a causal connexion from correlation and apprehending directly a causal connexion between pin-sticking and pain or contact with someone's hand and warmth. No doubt if you regularly get a headache after port wine you will conclude that port wine occasions headache; and again, you may accept your oculist's statement that the pain in your forehead is due to the fatigue of muscles in your eye. But both these cases are very different from the case of the pin; in the case of the pin there is no need for argument.

It is no doubt important in the case of the pin that the pain is "in the place where" the pin penetrates. But, even if we admit that this shows that the case is one of argument, it must be allowed that it is not argument from correlation only.

(ii) *The Correlation Argument.* Our knowledge of causal connexion in such cases as the pin is powerfully supported by the refined correlation between stimulation and sensation mentioned on p. 63.

[1] I am indebted to Miss Helen Smith for this consideration.

(iii) *The Explanation Argument.* Further there is nothing other than stimulation which can plausibly be suggested as the occasion of sensation. It is impossible to suggest, for example, that other mental events occasion sensations. There is no mental event which is regularly connected with the mental event *pleasure in food*. True this mental event is usually preceded by *desire for food*. But *desire for food* often occurs without being followed by *pleasure in food*, namely when no food is forthcoming. And *pleasure in food* sometimes occurs without being preceded by a *desire for food*.[1]

(iv) *The Inclusion Argument*.[2] Many people, who would deny that material facts can occasion or partly occasion mental facts, would yet admit that one mental fact can occasion another.[3] Thus the fact that I am annoyed now may be due to the fact that I have just observed that my house is smaller than yours. But my observation could not have occurred unless your house were larger than mine; for the observation includes as its object the fact that your house is larger than mine. Now if one complete, particular fact F_1 includes another F_2 as a constituent of itself, then anything which F_1 occasions is partly occasioned by F_2. Hence the fact that your house is larger than mine is part of what occasioned my annoyance. The fact about the houses is material and the annoyance, of course, is mental.

I conclude from these four arguments that material

---

[1] Broad, *The Mind and Its Place in Nature*, p. 114.
[2] I am indebted to Miss Cecily Wood for this argument.
[3] For this see next section.

events sometimes occasion or form part of the occasion of mental events.

3.22. Mental events sometimes occasion bodily events.

(i) *Inspection.* One might well say "I am angry with him because I heard him call me a fool". Such an occasioning by one mental event of another can be known without argument.[1] And suppose I am trying to decide whether to start work on a cross-word puzzle or to play golf and finally decide to do the cross-word puzzle. It seems to me that in such a case I know that the thinking involved in doing the cross-word puzzle was occasioned by my decision. It seems to me that I observe a causal relation between the two events. The two events in this case are both mental.

Suppose now that I decide instead to play golf. I am learning and so I describe to myself beforehand the movement I am about to make. It seems to me that I can observe that my decision to make that kind of movement was the occasion, or part of the occasion, of my making that kind of movement.[2]

This is an argument from an instance to the general statement that mental events sometimes occasion bodily events. It rests upon inspection of instances of deliberate movement.

[1] I am here again indebted to Miss Helen Smith. See also Johnson's *Logic*, II, 193. Perhaps the clearest case is where the hearing of a remark causes annoyance.

[2] One does not always carry out *just* the kind of movement one would like. The conditions no doubt are then unfavourable.

This appeal to inspection has been disputed by competent people.[1] These people have said that we cannot observe the occasioning of one event by another if that occasioning is indirect and involves intermediate events which are not observed. Now the immediate occasion of my movement is the contraction of my muscles; this contraction was occasioned by the passage of a nervous impulse down an efferent nerve fibre. The passage of this impulse was occasioned by a disturbance in the motor area of the cortex. This disturbance was, let us say, occasioned by my decision. But the disturbance was unobserved. Hence it cannot be claimed that I was able to observe the decision occasioning the disturbance, and no one has ever made such a claim. Hence, by the general principle with which we started, I could not have observed the decision occasioning the movement; for the decision occasioned the movement only via the unobserved disturbance.

Dr Broad has tried to answer this objection by claiming that, though we do not know directly that the decision is a *sufficient* cause for the movement, we may know directly that it is a *necessary* cause.

I can see that a decision is not a sufficient cause of movement. If I have recently become paralysed, I may decide to move my arm and fail to do so because of the defect in my nervous system. But I am afraid that we ought also to admit that the decision is not a direct necessary cause of the movement, i.e. that the decision is not even a part of the direct cause of the movement.

[1] Hume, *Enquiry Concerning Human Understanding*, Sect. VII Part I.

In spite of this I believe that in decision and movement I know without need of argument that there is a causal relation between the two. Of this doctrine Dr Broad says, "I should not care to assert that the doctrine in question is true; but I do think that it is plausible".[1] And later he says,

Is the connexion between cause and effect as mysterious and as little self-evident in the case of the voluntary production of voluntary movements as in all other cases? If so, we must hold that the first time a baby wills to move its hand it is just as much surprised to find its hand moving as it would be to find its leg moving or its nurse bursting into flames....It is perfectly plain that, in the case of volition and voluntary movement, there is a connexion between the cause and the effect which is not present in other cases[2] of causation, and which does make it plausible to hold that in this one case the nature of the effect can be foreseen by merely reflecting on the nature of the cause.

The inspection 'argument' is supported by two others.

(ii) *The Correlation Argument.* Many movements, such as running, are regularly preceded by certain decisions, and the nature of the movements varies with the nature of the decisions. This argument is supported by some of the correlations mentioned in the preceding section. For example, often there occurs first worry, then indigestion.

---

[1] *The Mind and Its Place in Nature,* pp. 101 and 102.

[2] Compare the case in which I am looking at the sky and a bird passes. The passing of the bird is the occasion of my observing the passing of the bird. And the effect contains the cause. See argument (iii) in the last section.

(iii) *The Watch Argument.* (*a*) There are many objects which have a very complex structure of a kind which makes them capable of satisfying desires. Watches and motor-cycles are such objects. (*b*) There is nothing in the nature of matter which tends to make it take up such complex and orderly patterns. Still less is there anything in the nature of matter which tends to make it arrange itself so as to satisfy human desires. (*c*) Therefore the occurrence of such orderly and desirable arrangements of matter as we find in the watch demand an explanation. (*d*) The best explanation is the usual one, namely that the desires influence through bodily movements the arrangement of material things. But, if so, then mental events occasion bodily events.

The full analysis of this argument, like the full analysis of the very similar argument from design to the existence of God, has not been adequately set out by logicians or philosophers. I could not even attempt to do so here. However, I venture a few remarks which are independent of the rest of the book, and may therefore be omitted if they seem a nuisance.

(α) Suppose that you found a great many pebbles so arranged as to form an edition of Shakespeare. This would surprise you and make you think that someone had arranged them so.

You would be surprised because, although that orderly and desirable arrangement is not less likely than any other particular arrangement, whether desirable or not, nevertheless the number of orderly and desirable arrangements is very much less than the number of disorderly and undesirable arrangements. Hence, assuming any particular arrangement to be as likely as any other, the probability of an orderly, desirable arrangement is much less than the probability of a disorderly and undesirable arrangement.

You would suppose that someone had arranged the pebbles because you would think this the best explanation of the surprising arrangement. Now why would you think so?

You would think it *an* explanation because the *antecedent* improbability of the existence of a mind and its interference with the pebbles is less than the *antecedent* improbability of such an orderly and desirable arrangement arising among the pebbles by chance, i.e. because of their own nature. By the 'antecedent probability' I mean the probability apart from the argument under discussion. Now why has the hypothesis *Mind has interfered with these pebbles* the antecedent probability which it has? Partly (1) because you think you know of similar cases in which a mind *has* been the explanation of such extraordinary material arrangements; and partly (2) because the hypothesis *Minds can interfere so as to produce desirable material arrangements and a mind has so interfered with these pebbles* has less *intrinsic* improbability than the desirable material arrangement. By the 'intrinsic probability' of the desirable material arrangement I mean the probability that a material arrangement will be desirable when one's only information is *Some material arrangement exists*. Similarly the intrinsic probability of *Some mind has desired and caused this arrangement* is the probability of *Some mind has desired and caused this arrangement* relative to the data *Minds exist*.

You think mental interference the *best* explanation because you cannot think of another with so high an antecedent probability.

(β) The argument from the watch to the conclusion *Mind interferes sometimes* is weaker than the argument from the pebbles or a watch to the conclusion *Here is another of those cases of the interference of mind.* For we cannot argue by analogy with *other cases* of the interference of mind to the antecedent probability of its interference in regard to the watch when the question at issue is "Do minds *ever* interfere?"

Hence the antecedent probability of the hypothesis of the interference of mind cannot, for *our* purpose, be assumed greater than its intrinsic probability. This considerably weakens this argument.

(γ) Broad suggests that watches and motor-cycles might be due to the action of our bodies without the action of mind. Complicated and desirable movements are carried out apparently without the aid of consciousness. For example, the complicated and desirable movements involved in the digestion of your last meal were successfully carried out without any interference from your mind. And, as Mr Mace says, what about the spider's web? Must we suppose that movements of the young and inexperienced spider spinning perfectly a web for the first time are prompted by consciousness?

And then we must remember that it looks very much as if many complicated and desirable arrangements of matter have occurred without the interference of mind; for example, leopards' bodies.

It might be replied that bodies so elaborate as to produce watches in response to the blows of the environment would themselves call for explanation quite as loudly as did the watches. And, as to the second point, it might be claimed that animal bodies *do* call for the interference of a mind, say the mind of God with life and happiness as his purpose, or the mind of the Devil with death and unhappiness as his purpose.

It seems to me: (1) That Dr Broad's suggestion and Mr Mace's instances of digestion and spiders' webs, emphasize the fact that the argument from desirable material arrangements is not a *demonstrative* argument but an argument which gives at most some probability to its conclusion. (2) That this argument's force is reduced by the existence of desirable arrangements due to the apparently automatic behaviour of complicated bodies which themselves arose *apparently* without the action of mind. But then to this it may be replied that such bodies need a Designer. We cannot further consider this here. (3) That the force of the watch argument is easily over-estimated, if one forgets that any inference to the interference of a mind as the explanation of a given object cannot be supported by analogy from other cases if the final question at issue is, "Does mind *ever* act on body?" (4) That, though this argument could not be of much use by itself, it considerably supports the conclusion already arrived at by the arguments from Inspection and Correlation—the conclusion that mind does act on body. For these other arguments provide the necessary antecedent probability.

(iv) *The Telegram Argument.* (*Unsound.*) Like circumstances produce like effects. When you receive first a telegram "Our son is dead" and then a telegram "Your son is dead", the material circumstances are very similar; they differ only in the presence of the mark 'Y'. If, therefore, the material circumstances are the only causes of your behaviour after receiving these telegrams, then your behaviour should be very similar after each. But it is not. Therefore there are other circumstances, viz. mental ones, which are part of the cause of your behaviour.

The premiss, *The material circumstances are very similar in each case of telegram reception and reaction,* is quite unwarranted. The obvious material circumstances are similar. But the hidden material circumstances on which the obvious ones act before producing the behaviour are very different. One telegram starts an impulse which takes one path through the nervous system, and the other telegram starts a nervous impulse which takes a very different path involving very different nerve cells. Hence very different reactions may be expected from a consideration of the material circumstances alone. There are machines on Brighton pier which respond well to pennies but ignore halfpennies, and there are machines on railway platforms which react to sixpences with chocolates and to shillings with cigarettes.

3.3. ARGUMENTS AGAINST OCCASIONING.

(i) *The Conservation of Energy Argument.* This argument is based upon the scientific doctrine of the Conservation of Energy and a general statement about causation. It runs as follows:

(*a*) The material world as a whole never gains or loses energy.

(*b*) If a change in X occasions a change in Y then energy passes from X into Y.

From (*b*) it follows (α) that, if a bodily event were to occasion a mental event, then energy from the material world would pass into the mental world; and (β) that, if a mental event were to occasion a bodily event, then energy would pass from the mental world into the material world.

But by (*a*) both these things are impossible.

Therefore neither do bodily events occasion mental events nor mental events bodily events.

An argument based on general premisses, such as (*a*) and (*b*), which gives results in conflict with what we seem to know by inspection, should always be regarded with the greatest suspicion. But this argument is ancient and respectable. It is *valid*, i.e. it involves no formal fallacy or linguistic confusion, so that *if* the premisses are true, the conclusion must be. And it appears well-founded, i.e. its premisses are plausible. We must therefore give it attention in spite of its unfortunate conclusion.

Its first premiss is the Law of the Conservation of Energy. One may dispute it only as a last resort. The changes in the world involve, of course, frequent and tremendous redistributions of energy. For example, you go for a ride on your bicycle and lose energy fast. But this energy is to be found in the form of heat and of movement among the particles of the air through which you have passed. So that always what is lost on the swings is gained on the round-abouts.

The second premiss is much more doubtful. It may be admitted that, within the material world, if a change in X occasions a change in Y then energy passes from X to Y.[1] But this will not prove that if mind acts on body then the body gains energy. The more sweeping proposition, *Whether X and Y are material or not, if a change in X occasions a change in Y then energy passes from X to Y,* would prove that if mind acts on body then the body gains energy. But is this sweeping proposition self-evident, or is it known in some other way? It is not self-evident. And the only other way in which it could be known is by finding that in many various cases of the interaction of body and mind, energy always passed. But this would involve admitting that there *is* interaction between body and mind.

This argument against interaction is therefore, after all, ill-founded.

(ii) *The Conditioned-Reflex Argument.* We have seen that purposive movements take place even when not occasioned by a mental event. The frog with cerebral

---

[1] Dr Broad disputes even this. He says the changes in the direction and velocity of the movement of the weight in a pendulum are caused by the pull of its string. But I do not feel quite happy about this case. Can we say that changes in the string *occasion* changes in the movement of the weight. Is it not merely that the relationship between weight and string is one of the *conditions* of the changes? See *The Mind and Its Place in Nature*, p. 107.

hemispheres removed, and therefore presumably without consciousness, makes purposive movements if acid is placed on the skin. You digest your food without consciousness. Nobody thinks it necessary to attribute consciousness to the spider when he spins his web.

And recently it has been shown that that kind of behaviour commonly judged the most conclusive evidence for consciousness, namely learning, may take place without the action of consciousness. Take a starved dog and place meat on his tongue; this will occasion saliva to flow. This is a reflex act; that is, decision does not occasion it; it would take place even if the cerebral hemispheres were removed. Stimulate the saliva reflex in this way one hundred times, and ring a bell each time you present the meat. Finally ring the bell without presenting the meat; this will then occasion saliva to flow. Thus, it is concluded, the dog has learned the 'meaning' of the bell without the use of consciousness.

Now the whole of the nervous system consists of a tremendous number of reflex arcs. And the nervous processes accompanying so-called deliberate action do not differ in kind from those accompanying reflex action; they differ only in complexity. Therefore the belief that mental events are necessary for deliberate actions but not for reflex actions is quite unjustifiable.

We have already considered the facts mentioned in this argument and tried to assess their bearing on the question whether mental events occasion bodily events. A few further remarks may be made here.

(1) The importance of the data about conditioned reflexes has been much exaggerated. These data show

that a reaction hitherto produced only by one kind of stimulus may come to be produced by another without that reaction having been caused by foresight and decision. But it has not been shown that a new stimulus can come to be effective without the action of consciousness. Conditioned reflexes have not been set up in an animal without cerebral hemispheres. Would the bell have come to have its salivary effect if the dog had not heard it or not been hungry? We do not know. Before the work on conditioned reflexes we did not know that consciousness was necessary to the establishing of new stimuli. And now we do not know that it is unnecessary.

It may be claimed that before the 'discovery' of conditioned reflexes it had been supposed that no 'learning' took place unless the reaction was due to foresight and decision. But is this true? Surely everyone knew that a child, at first unafraid of snakes, might come to shiver in its shoes and raise its hair at the sight of a snake. And shivering in the shoes and rising of the hair are not acts due to decision; they are reflexes. So we knew of conditioned reflexes before Pavlov told us about those which he established in his dogs. (Not but what his work is extremely valuable and suggestive for psychology.)

(2) It is worth mentioning that *new* reaction to *old* stimulus more strongly suggests the interference of mind than does *old* reaction to *new* stimulus. Thus Kolher's ape first tried to get fruit, which had been placed outside his cage, by means of a single bamboo stick (an old reaction). This failed and he fitted a second stick into the first (new reaction) and reached the food this way.

(3) The facts about the frog (p. 60) and the spider's spinning prove at most that purposive behaviour is not always due to consciousness; and therefore that an argument from purposive behaviour to consciousness does not *demonstrate* its conclusion. It does not follow that such an argument never lends any probability to its conclusion. Much less does it follow that that conclusion is false or unjustified by any other arguments, namely inspection and correlation, which support this conclusion.

3.4. CONCLUSION. Bodily events do occasion mental events and mental events do occasion bodily events.

CHAPTER VI

DO BODILY EVENTS PRODUCE MENTAL EVENTS?

1. **Meaning of Production.** The doctrine that material events may produce mental events may be restated in other ways. We may say: "Material events and material facts may form the complete explanation of a mental event". Or we may say: "Material conditions, together with certain material changes, may be the whole cause of a mental event". Thus it may be suggested that the existence of a certain kind of complicated nervous system (material condition) together with a certain kind of intensity of stimulation of that system (material occasion) might be a sufficient explanation of a mental event—say a feeble sensation to begin with. Such a nervous system, it may be said, would "secrete thought as the liver secretes bile". Such a system, so stimulated, would not cause that primordial sensation by acting upon a mind. Such a system, so stimulated, would create, or rather produce, the sensation out of nothing.

I write the phrase 'out of nothing' because I think it is a legitimate expression for the very peculiar kind of change which this theory involves. It may be contrasted with the sort of change which occurs on the view that bodily events are only the occasion of mental events. According to this theory a bodily event may affect a previously existing mind; it will affect it in that the mind which was manifesting a generic character, consciousness, in *one* specific form will begin to manifest it in *another* specific form. For example, you are reading, when your ear is stimulated by the vibrations set up by an explosion; this stimulation occasions a change from your reading-consciousness to a terrified listening-consciousness. This is the sort of change we are used to. Things change in that they have first one specific form of a generic quality or relation and then another specific form of the *same* generic quality or relation. Thus a coat may change from black to green, and it may shrink; but it is always coloured and always has some size. Again, a piece of plasticine may be moulded first into a dog and then into an elephant and be dyed pink. But it will still be the same piece of plasticine provided it neither loses its *generic* characters, *has some size and shape* and *is coloured*, nor gains some new *generic* character, such as consciousness.

If purely material circumstances produced the primordial sensation, this was not a change of the orthodox sort. For sensation is a species of consciousness. And, if the preceding circumstances were purely material, they could not contain a manifestation of consciousness. Nor could they contain a generic character of which consciousness is a specific form; for, as we have seen, consciousness is itself supremely generic and not a species of some other character, especially a spatial or extensive character.

Notice also that, associated with this peculiar kind of change, is a peculiar kind of causation. Usually the manifestation of one set of specific forms of certain generic qualities and relations, say masses and distances, is caused and explained by a previous manifestation of the same generic qualities and relations. But, if mental events are produced by purely material events, this rule is broken.

2. Do Material Events produce Mental Events and vice versa? This is our question III.

2.1. EMPIRICAL ARGUMENTS. (*a*) The mental event of deciding to make a certain movement does not produce that movement. For something besides the decision is necessary, and this something is the material circumstance of a sound nervous system. This is obvious when a recently paralysed man decides to do something, forgetting his paralysis, and fails to do it.

(*b*) Certain experimental facts suggest, though they do not prove, that for sensation something besides stimulation is necessary and that this something is a mental circumstance, namely what may be described as the presence of a mind with 'free' attention. For the hypnotized subject, if told that he will feel nothing in his left arm, feels nothing even when pricked with a pin. And when we are fighting we do not feel slight wounds. It may be that hypnosis and excitement cause a peculiar condition of the nervous system which prevents the passage of a nervous impulse from the wounded skin to the brain. If this is so, there is not in these cases stimulation without sensation. Still I mention the facts for what they are worth.

2.2. PHILOSOPHICAL ARGUMENT AGAINST PRODUC-TION. It has been asserted that the production of mental events by bodily events and vice versa are both impossible.

2.21. The reason for this assertion has usually been stated very badly. Some people have said, "The cause must be like its effect. Mind is too unlike matter for the one to influence the other". But this will not do. Some effects are very unlike their causes. The revolution of the wheels of a car is very unlike the explosion of a gas. This kind of unlikeness is not the kind meant by those people who have said, "Mind is unlike matter". But then they have not said *what* kind of unlikeness they *do* mean; consequently they must expect answers which are beside their 'real' point. And some people have said, "If one event is to cause another, then they must fall within the same system and be part of the same unity".[1] This statement is so vague that it is useless as it stands. Professor Stout has tried in *Mind and Matter* to put in a clearer way the doctrine so miserably expressed in the two statements we have just considered.

2.22. Stout holds that material events and conditions cannot *produce* mental events. In other words, Stout holds that material events and conditions could never *completely explain* a mental event. This doctrine he seeks to prove as follows:

(i) An analysis of what is meant by 'causation' and

[1] Broad in *The Mind and Its Place in Nature* has tried to explain what is meant by this. I do not find his explanation adequate. I believe his *two* philosophical arguments to be the *one* offered by Stout and based on the *Generic Resemblance Principle*; see p. 89.

'explanation' reveals that, though the circumstances which provide the explanation of a state of affairs may differ ever so much in detail from that state of affairs, there must nevertheless be a generic likeness between what is explained and what explains it. Production of mind by matter, therefore, since it is explanation without generic likeness, is a self-contradictory conception.

(ii) An analysis of change reveals that between the successive temporal slices of a change there must be not only unlikeness, but also a generic likeness. Stout says,[1] "When anything changes, it does so always in *some respect*. The change affects some general aspect of its nature, and its successive phases consist in specific and particular variations of this generic character". Production of mind by matter, therefore, since it is a change without generic likeness, is a self-contradictory conception.

2.23. Let us consider these arguments. To begin with the last. I can see that all change *in a thing* involves generic likeness between successive stages. But I do not feel confident that all change is change in a thing. Suppose that a new generic character which had hitherto characterised nothing in any form burst into being. That would be a change and no mistake. And I see no *logical* impossibility, nothing self-contradictory, about such an event. It would perhaps be necessarily an unexplained event, but that is the different claim of the first argument; we must now examine it.

[1] *Mind and Matter*, p. 132. See also p. 134, line 26.

2.24. The argument from the analysis of explanation rests upon (*a*) the statement that there is not a generic likeness between a mental event and a material event, and (*b*) a statement about the analysis of explanation.

2.241. We must agree that (*a*) there is no character which is specified both in *is conscious* and *has an extensive quality*; there is no highly generic character of which both these are species. The peaceful progress of two automobiles is unlike the resulting collision. But the progress, though unlike the collision, has a generic resemblance to it; both consist in the movement of extended coloured, etc., objects. And hearing words is unlike the anger it may cause; yet both are species of consciousness. But, if consciousness were to result from the movements of brain molecules, there would be no generic resemblance between cause and effect.

2.242. The statement (*b*) about the analysis of explanation, upon which Stout's argument rests, may be more explicitly stated as follows: *If one situation S explains another S' then S and S' must be manifestations*[1] *of specific forms of the same generic qualities and relations.* This may be restated in our vocabulary as follows: *If a set of facts, S, is the cause of a set of facts, S', then the components (the qualities and relations) in the set S must specify the same generic characters as are specified in the components of the set S'.* If we call generic characters *variables* and their specific forms their *values* and com-

---

[1] "Red is manifested in this event" does not mean "In this event red is manifested to someone". It means, "Red is component in this event".

pletely generic characters *supreme variables*, then we can express this principle conveniently as follows: *If S explains S' then they must be manifestations of the same supreme variables.*[1] This may be called the Principle of Generic Resemblance. Such a principle, if true, would be important. Let us apply it to instances.

Suppose we know a law to the effect that, whenever the glucose in the blood in a body is insufficient, then a desire for sugar will arise in the mind which owns the body; and also that there is insufficient glucose in the blood of John Smith. We shall be able to predict a desire for sugar in John Smith's mind. But can we say that we have explained this desire for sugar? Would not such an explanation be unsatisfactory? It would be unsatisfactory in a way in which a psychological explanation would not be. If we know that John Smith loves Arabella and believes that only sugar will save her life, we have a satisfactory explanation of his desire to get hold of some sugar. We can see how a love for Arabella and belief that she needed sugar would lead to desire for sugar. In the psychological account we see, to use Professor Stout's phrase, *how* the consequent follows from the antecedent. In the physiological account we know *that* the consequent follows the antecedent, but we cannot see *how*; in the physiological account we have, to use Professor Stout's phrase, "just one damn thing after another". This, as Mr Mace points out to me, is one reason why people say that Freud, with his psychological

[1] As Professor Broad has pointed out to me, it is highly important here to see exactly what is meant by 'supreme variable'. Cf. p. 175, note 1.

explanations, was the first man "to take determinism seriously in psychology".

Mechanical explanations of mechanical situations approximate most nearly to perfect explanation. We can see how the configuration and velocities of a set of particles at one time arise from the configuration and velocities of those particles at an earlier time. And, if a body were to move at a certain speed and in a certain direction *in vacuo* for one period, that would explain its moving at the same speed and in the same direction during the next period.

On the other hand, mechanical facts (spatio-temporal facts) would never explain why a thing is green or has such and such a smell. We might know that, whenever particles are moving in such and such a way, then there will be something green. This would enable us to predict. But it would not enable us to explain. For colour, hardness and warmth, though extensive,[1] are not themselves spatio-temporal characters, as are specific sizes, shapes, distances and motions. Given hydrogen and oxygen and a spark, we can predict water, but we do not in this way explain its occurrence.

2.243. I state here by anticipation the results of the discussion in the next section (2.244) because that discussion is a little complicated. It may be omitted if its results, as stated below, are assumed. In section 2.244 I conclude that the Principle of Generic Resemblance between Cause and Effect must be accepted.

And I conclude that the Principle of Continuity is

[1] See p. 19. And see *Mind and Matter*, p. 130.

even more certainly to be accepted. This principle may be stated as follows: *In so far as there is generic resemblance between two situations there must also be generic likeness between their effects.* This principle does not assert generic resemblance between cause and effect; it asserts generic resemblance between the effects of generically like causes.

2.244. It must be admitted that the principle of generic resemblance between cause and effect is not without plausibility. We must, however, distinguish two principles, the first of which I believe I can clearly see to be true and the second of which I think I see to be true rather less clearly. The first is the Principle of Continuity, and the second is a compound principle containing the Principle of the Generic Resemblance of the Cause and the Principle of the Generic Resemblance of the Effect.

I. The Principle of Continuity. Like causes produce like effects—this principle concerning causation no one doubts. And knowing this I think we can see two further principles: (i) Specifically like causes produce specifically like effects; and (ii) Generically like causes produce generically like effects. This latter statement is the Principle of Continuity. It may be more accurately stated as follows: If one set of values of a set of variables causes a manifestation of a set of values of the same or a different set of variables, then any other set of values of the first variables will also cause a set of values of the second set of variables. Symbolically: If $v_1 \ldots v_n$ values of $V_1 \ldots V_n$ cause $v_1' \ldots v_n'$ values of $V_1' \ldots V_n'$, then every set of values of $V_1 \ldots V_n$ will cause a set of values of $\dot{V_1}' \ldots V_n'$, where $V_1 \ldots V_n$ may or may not be identical with $V_1' \ldots V_n'$.[1] For example, if a speed of 10 m.p.h. causes wind resistance, then a speed of 20 m.p.h. will also cause wind resistance—a higher degree in point of fact. A speed of 50 million m.p.h. causes heat only because a speed of 1 m.p.h. has the same effect though in a negligible degree. Again, it is not merely that at some temperatures an increase in temperature causes change in the length of a metal rod; this happens at all temperatures. Indeed the statements of dependence to which the scientist allows the name of law are all concerned with *all* values of the variables between which the dependence holds (see pp. 9 and 37). The apparent exceptions[2] only make clearer what is stated in this Principle of Continuity. Thus, up to a certain point, more weight at the end of a piece of elastic increases its length, but beyond a certain point the effect is no longer similar; for the elastic breaks. But the new situation, though dissimilar in respect of a relatively specific variable, is still a material situation; and the exact position of the broken threads is predictable by the general laws of physics stated in terms of supremely generic variables such as space, time and mass. Similarly, as we saw, the

[1] And we might add "where $v_1 \ldots v_n$ may or may not be identical with $v_1' \ldots v_n'$", in order to cover cases of unchanged state where the first stage reproduces itself exactly in the second and the second in the third.

[2] Some apparent exceptions will require very careful treatment. Broad's articles on Demonstrative Induction, *Mind*, Vol. xxxix, will be found useful.

monotonous movement of two cars may suddenly result in a collision. But though the collision situation is specifically unlike the previous effects of the work of the car engines, it is generically similar to those previous effects. In the collision no new supremely generic variable manifests itself.

Thus we see that in so far as the causes remain generically similar the effects also remain generically similar. We are able to see that the universal generic causal facts which the scientist discovers, approximate more and more to forms which obey this principle of continuity. Such supremely generic causal generalizations as are expressed in the laws of motion and Maxwell's equations, are easily seen to fulfil it exactly.

All this I think enables us to know that causal process in this world does in fact obey the principle of continuity. I cannot feel sure that the analysis of explanation requires the truth of this principle—perhaps it does. But I do submit that somehow we know that this principle in fact holds of the explanations in this world. And it seems very doubtful whether induction and scientific argument would be possible unless it were true.

II. The Principles of Resemblance. (i) The Resemblance of the Cause: If one situation S forms the complete explanation of another S', then every supremely generic variable manifested in S must also be manifested in S'. Symbolically: If an effect situation manifests $v_1' \ldots v_n'$ values of supreme variables $V_1' \ldots V_n'$, then amongst its causes must be found some value of V_1', some value of $V_2' \ldots$ some value of V_n'.

(ii) The Resemblance of the Effect. If one situation S'

is the complete effect of a situation S, then every supreme variable manifested in S must also be manifested in S'. Symbolically: If a cause-situation manifests $v_1 \ldots v_n$ values of supreme variables $V_1 \ldots V_n$, then amongst the things to which that situation is causally relevant must be a manifestation of V_1 and a manifestation of $V_2 \ldots$ and a manifestation of V_n. The principles are roughly equivalent to the statement that in the causal process supremely generic characters are neither (i) gained, nor (ii) lost.

I do not find these principles as certain as the principle of continuity. Nevertheless, I think that consideration will enable us to see that these principles also are true. Perhaps some of the examples immediately above suggest exceptions to these principles in that values of one variable appear to cause values of another variable. But a little care reveals that this is a mistake. We might say loosely that heating causes lengthening; but really temperature and length at one time cause temperature and length at another. It is not that, because of an alteration in temperature, a world formerly containing nothing having length comes to contain something having length. And all the variables mentioned in physical and chemical laws have always been manifested in some specific form or other. Not only is it impossible that certain spatio-temporal values should result in colours and temperatures while others should not (principle of continuity), it is also impossible that the occurrence of colour or temperature should ever be explained by a set of purely spatio-temporal facts. And we saw above that psychological facts seem to require psychological explanation. No one anticipates for a moment that some new supreme variable will begin to be manifested. Much less certainly, no one anticipates that some supreme variable manifested up till now will cease to be manifested. This is not because we can see that such a change is logically impossible; nor on the other hand is it merely a matter of habit. It is because we somehow know that this world is a causal system having generic continuity.

2.245. If we accept the principles of resemblance, we must reject the view that mental events are produced by material situations. For consciousness, as we have admitted, would be a supreme new variable.

And even if we accept only the milder principle of continuity we must reject the doctrine of production unless we are prepared to say that *every* material event produces a mental event. For the material events which happen in a brain when it is stimulated do not differ in kind, but only in complexity, from those which take place elsewhere, for example in your kettle when it boils. They therefore, by the principle of continuity, cannot have some entirely new kind of effect.

We do not know for certain that there is not a universal association of mental and material events. Indeed, it is very difficult to draw the line between those material events which are accompanied by consciousness and those which are not. But is it likely that every movement of the sand on the Sahara, every wave on the coasts of the northern shores of Australia, is associated with its own modification of someone's consciousness? And, if not, we may argue against production, not merely from the principles of resemblance, but also from the principle of continuity.

Stout accepts the universal correlation of mental and material events. He cannot therefore argue from the principle of continuity against the doctrine that brain events produce mental events. *He* rejects such production because it conflicts with the principles of resemblance.

3. **Stout's Argument against Occasioning.**[1] Stout wishes to go further and to maintain that there is no causal connexion between bodily and mental events.[2]

It must be noticed to begin with that neither the principle of continuity nor the principles of resemblance have any tendency whatever to prove this conclusion. Another principle, easily confused with the principle of the resemblance of the cause, would lead to this conclusion. But then the principle is false, and I cannot think that Stout would maintain it. This is the principle that any event which shares in causing an event E, must manifest some supreme variable manifested in E. In other words, not only must the events which together make up the whole cause of E manifest *between* them every supreme variable manifested in E, but each of these events *severally* must manifest every supreme variable manifested in E.

From this it follows that anything which shares in causing a mental event, must itself be mental. But I see no reason to accept the principle from which this surprising conclusion follows. From the principle of the

[1] Section 3 may be omitted.   [2] See p. 97, note 1.

resemblance of the cause it follows that among the facts to which a mental fact is due must be at least one mental fact. And from the principle of the resemblance of the effect it follows that among the facts which a material fact, such as a brain disturbance following on stimulation, shares in causing, must be a material fact. But neither of these deductions conflicts with our earlier result that decisions occasion or partly occasion movements and that brain disturbances occasion or partly occasion sensations.

This earlier result seems far more certain than this last principle which conflicts with it. I am sure that the sticking of a pin into my finger is causally relevant to the pain which regularly follows. And I am sure that my decision to bowl an off-break is causally relevant to my subsequent movement.[1] On the other hand, I deny the principle that if a set of values of variables $V_1 \ldots V_n$, cause another set of values $V_1 \ldots V_n$, then the effect value of any one of these, V_{n-m}, is fixed wholly by the

---

[1] I doubt now whether this argument is relevant against Stout. Mr George Paul has pointed out to me that it is unfair to say that Stout denies any causal connexion between sensory disturbance and subsequent sensation. Stout would allow that the plain man, when he says "I felt a stab of pain because you stuck that pin into me", speaks truly.

What Stout would deny is that the pin-puncturing is part of the explanation of the pain, in the sense in which a collision is part of the explanation of the movement of a billiard ball. He would say that the connexion between the pin-puncturing and the pain is as follows: The pin-puncturing occasions nervous and finally cerebral disturbance; the cerebral disturbance is one *aspect of* a concrete event whose other *aspect* is the pain.

cause value of that same variable so that all the rest are irrelevant to it. Not only previous length but also temperature is relevant to the length of a metal rod, and not only temperature but also pressure is relevant to the volume of a gas.

Stout has, however, a different and positive reason for maintaining that there is no causal connexion between bodily and mental events. He would say:

> The correlations you have so laboriously set out are, as you say, due to a necessary connexion between body and mind. But this connexion is logical, not causal. You say that the correlation between a pin-prick and pain is due to the fact that the pin-prick starts an afferent impulse which causes a brain disturbance which causes the pain. But the brain disturbance does not cause the pain. It never, indeed, occurs without the pain; but this is because the material event, the brain disturbance, can not, by a logical necessity, occur without the pain.
>
> The logical necessity here is not *formal* logical necessity. The occurrence of the brain disturbance does not necessitate the occurrence of the pain in the sense in which the fact *Every aesthete is incapable and everyone who is incapable is malicious* necessitates *Every aesthete is malicious*. The fact that the brain is in such and such a state necessitates that the mind is in such and such a state, in that sense of 'necessitates' in which *This is blue* necessitates *This has a surface*, i.e. *This is extended*.

Every material event so necessitates a mental event and vice versa.

It is easy to see the distinction between this sort of necessity and causal necessity. In order to get from London to Paris a man must cross the Channel. But this is only a causal necessity; it does not hold in fairy-land, for in fairyland people may disappear in London and reappear in Paris without passing over the Channel. Again, if you stab a man through the heart he cannot live. But this is only a causal impossibility: in a dream he could live and often does, and in a world where causal laws were different from those of this world he would live. On the other hand, if a thing is red, it must be of some size, however small, and if a thing is triangular it must be three-sided, and if a thing is hard it must be extended. Not even in fairyland or dreams do these rules break down. A breakdown of the connexion between arsenic and death would be surprising and causally impossible. A breakdown of the connexion between redness and extendedness would be absurd and, in a sense, logically impossible. I think that Stout would say that every material event necessitates a mental event and vice versa because each *completes* the other in the way in which *This has size* completes *This is blue*. There cannot be spatial characters without extensive characters to fill the space and there cannot be material characters (combination of spatial and extensive characters) without consciousness.

Stout is fully aware that this completion of materiality in mentality or consciousness and vice versa, is less obvious at first than the completion of an extensive fact, e.g. *This is red*, in a purely spatial fact, e.g. *This has a surface* and vice versa.[1] But he claims that it becomes obvious on reflection.

I gather that it becomes obvious that material events

[1] See *Mind and Matter*, p. 154.

need mental events when we consider what is called their 'dynamic' character. If we consider merely a material *fact*, e.g. *This is red and round*, it is far from obvious that it needs a mental fact. But if we consider material *events*, such as a sandstorm or a wave, and how their earlier stages cause their later stages, how one body of water *pushes* another, then we see the need for consciousness. For a proper analysis of pushing, forcing, cannot be given without reference to consciousness and wanting.

I gather that it is in consciousness of self that it becomes obvious that mental events need and are completed in material events. Here, just as we are not aware of one thing as extended and of another as blue, so we are aware not of one thing as conscious and of another as material, but of consciousness as embodied. If a man strikes you in the back you do not say, "He struck the back of the body which this mind owns"; you say, "He struck me".

I need not say that this is not an adequate account of Stout's analysis and defence of his view. Until Stout's own account is studied no judgment can be passed. But for myself, I cannot, at present at any rate, see that what he says is true. I cannot see that 'pushing' and 'forcing', as applied to material things, include in their definition reference to consciousness.

Stout, of course, does not mean that when a growing plant pushes aside the soil, that plant itself has a mind. He thinks it *may* have a mind; and, if so, then the pushing by the plant is like the pushing of a man or an animal and includes a wishing. He also thinks that, if the plant has not a mind, then it is a part of something which has a mind; in this case the pushing by the plant is comparable to one of my hands (part of my body which body has a mind) pushing the other. Inanimate material things perhaps are connected with a mind which animates the whole of so-called inanimate nature. The individual material things are then connected with mind only in the secondary sense in which my hand, as opposed to my whole body, is connected with mind.

But I cannot see that there is even this secondary reference to consciousness in the transactions of material things, such as the breaking of a tree by the wind.

Nor can I see that mental events need to be completed in material events. Even if we suppose that consciousness occupies space in a sense at least analogous to that in which colours and temperatures do, need we suppose that the space is also occupied by extensive qualities?

And, even if this were necessary, should we have to allow that every change in consciousness necessitates a change in those material qualities. Although colour necessitates size, there is not a change in shape and size for every change in colour.

And, even if consciousness requires material events as objects for consciousness (see App. 1), this is very different from claiming that my sensation of red requires the cerebral disturbance which is usually supposed to occasion it.

In a word, I am not convinced that mentality needs to be completed in materiality, nor am I convinced that materiality needs to be completed in mentality. And, even if there is this logical connexion, I do not see that it precludes a causal connexion.

4. **Summary.** We have been concerned with three propositions:

I. Bodily events and mental events are causally connected.

II. Bodily events are sometimes the occasion or part of the occasion of mental events and vice versa.

III. Material events produce, that is, explain without the necessity of any other conditions, mental events and vice versa.

I and II we accept. They are well supported by inspection and arguments from the correlations between body and mind.

Stout rejects I and II on the ground that the necessary connexion between bodily and mental events is not causal but a case of a universal logical connexion between material and mental events.[1]

III we deny. For we do not accept a universal association between material and mental events and, by the principle of continuity, we cannot say that some material events, namely brain events, suffice to cause mental events, while others which do not differ from them in kind, cause no mental events whatever.

Besides, III conflicts with the principle of generic resemblance between cause and effect.

Stout also denies III. He cannot do so from our first reason, but he does so from our second.

[1] See p. 97, note 1.

CHAPTER VII

OWNERSHIP

We must now see how these propositions I, II and III are relevant to the philosophical problem of the relation between body and mind. We defined this as the problem of the analysis of that relation which holds between X's body and X's mind which he expresses by calling a certain body his own. The relevance of I, II and III to philosophical theories about the analysis of *ownership* will be obvious when these theories are stated. These theories are Interactionism, Parallelism, Epiphenomenalism, the Double-Aspect theory, and Stout's theory. Before stating these theories I must explain that 'interactionism' and 'parallelism', besides being used as names for philosophic theories, have also sometimes been used as names for two mild non-philosophical propositions. 'Parallelism', in the mild sense, is the proposition that for every mental event there is a bodily event which always accompanies it. 'Interactionism', in the mild sense, is the proposition that some material events occasion mental events and vice versa, in fact proposition II above. Interactionism, in this mild sense, we have accepted. Parallelism, in the mild sense, is unproved but plausible. We may now pass to the statement of the philosophical theories.

1. **Interactionism.** This theory may be stated in the following four propositions:

(i) The mind and the body are two things—like a cooking stove and a kettle.

(ii) Each is capable of existing without the other.

(iii) But throughout life they interact on one another. In other words, certain states of the one act on the other so as to form the occasion of certain states in the other. Thus stimulation of the body occasions sensation, and decision occasions movement. Similarly heat in the stove occasions the boiling of the kettle, and the over-boiling of the kettle occasions the rusting of the stove. A condition in each case is the previous proximity of the kettle and the stove.

(iv) "Mind *M owns* body *B*" means, "Between *M* and *B* there holds the particular sort of intimate causal connexions indicated by the correlations outlined in Chap. iv".

2. **Parallelism.** This theory may be stated as follows:

(i) The mind and the body are two things.

(ii) Each is capable of existing without the other.

(iii) Throughout life the states of the one run parallel with the states of the other. That is, for each kind of mental state there is just one kind of bodily state which always accompanies it and vice versa. But neither do bodily states influence mental nor mental bodily. The hands of your clock move as the sun moves. But the movements of the one do not cause the movements of the other nor are they joint effects of a common cause.

(iv) "*M owns B*" means, "Between *M* and *B* there holds the double parallelism mentioned in (iii)—every bodily event in B has a mental companion in M and vice versa".

3. **Epiphenomenalism.** This may be stated as follows:

(i) The body is a thing but the mind is not. The mind is not a thing, but a string of events which do not form a thing. Each of these events is produced and completely explained by some bodily event. We may say that the mental events are like the shadows a body casts or the smells a factory makes; but neither analogy is satisfactory.[1]

(ii) The body can exist without the mind but not the mind without the body.

(iii) Bodily events have effects. Mental events have none.

(iv) "M owns B" means, "M is a string of events *produced* by events in B". These events which make up M are not events in the life history of a thing, M, caused by the action of B on M. There is no second thing M. M is a series of by-products of the activity of B.

4. **The Double-Aspect Theory.** This theory may be stated as follows:

(i) The mind and the body are not two things. They are 'aspects of' something which is neither the body nor the mind. I do not know at all clearly what is meant by this. The best I can do is to suggest the following

---

[1] "…as the steam-whistle which accompanies the work of a locomotive engine without influence on its machinery" (Huxley: Essay "Automata"). (Quoted by Miss B. Edgell, *Mental Life* p. 261.)

analogy. Suppose that you walk between two rows of mirrors. There will then be two series of reflections of you; the one series will appear in the left-hand row of mirrors, the other series in the right-hand row. Neither of these series forms the history of a *thing*. The only things concerned are you and the mirrors.

(ii) The mind could not exist without the body.

(iii) The states of the mind parallel the states of the body. But they do not act on one another (cf. Interactionism). On the other hand, the parallelism is not an ultimate fact. It occurs because bodily and mental events are joint effects of a common cause.

(iv) "*M owns B*" means, "*M* and *B* are series of events which are 'aspects of' the same thing in the sense explained in (i) and (iii)".

5. **Stout's Theory of Body and Mind.** It is impossible to give here a proper exposition of this theory. Stout rejects epiphenomenalism on the grounds that it involves production. 'Parallelism' and 'interactionism', if used as names for the mild and scientific statements mentioned on p. 103, Stout accepts. Parallelism, in this sense, is the statement that every sort of mental event does not occur without a characteristic bodily correlate and vice versa. Interactionism, in this sense, is the statement that some mental events cannot occur without certain bodily events and vice versa. "Now", Stout says, "there must be some reason why the events in my mind parallel the events in *my* body and not the body of someone else; and there must be some reason why the events in my mind cannot occur without certain

events in *my* body occurring also, though they may occur without the occurrence of such events in someone *else's* body." Hence the relations between bodily events and mental events stated, and stated truly, in parallelism and interactionism in their mild scientific forms, imply some other relation between these events. This relation is probably the one which we express by calling some pairs of events 'events in the life history of one person'. Hence both scientific parallelism and scientific interactionism imply and do not analyse ownership. Therefore, when to scientific parallelism we add the statement, *And this correlation between a set of bodily events and a set of mental events is the relation of ownership*, thus making a philosophic theory of parallelism, then we speak falsely. Similarly, if we claim that the necessary connexion between bodily events and mental events is the relation of ownership, thus obtaining philosophic interactionism, then again we speak falsely. For the parallelism and necessary connexion are both *dependent upon* ownership.

The proper definition of 'ownership' is in terms of *completion*. Every material event is completed in a mental event and vice versa, just as every spatial event, e.g. *This's being round*, is completed in some extensive event, e.g. *This's being red*, or *This's being warm*. You cannot have a surface which is neither coloured nor hot nor cold nor hard nor soft, etc. Similarly, you cannot have disembodied mind. There is a kind of logical connexion between mentality and materiality.

Now, if you take a set of material events which form a body and a set of mental events which form a mind, and the members of each set complete each other, then the mind is said to *own* the body and the body to be *animated* by the mind.

6. Conclusion.

(*A*) Epiphenomenalism is false. For it involves production. And we rejected production in rejecting proposition III of Chap. VI.

(*B*) The Double-Aspect Theory is false. For bodily and mental events are not merely joint effects of a common cause. They have a lineal causal connexion, by proposition II of Chap. VI. Besides, the Double-Aspect Theory involves a third and completely mysterious parallel series of events which produce the bodily and mental events.

(*C*) Parallelism is false. For there is a causal connexion between bodily and mental events, by propositions I and II of Chap. VI. And, as Stout argues, if changes in one thing run parallel with changes in another, it is always because there is some other relation between the two things besides that of having parallel states. Thus, the two faces of a railway clock are *attached to the same mechanism*. And this other relation will surely be either identical with the relation of ownership or involved in its definition.

(*D*) Interactionism will not quite do. For, as Stout argues, if changes in one thing very often occasion changes in another, it is always because there is some other relation between the two things besides that of interaction. The other relation is usually that of proximity. Thus the kettle and stove in our example interacted because of proximity. In the case of the interaction of a body and a mind, the interaction appears to be due to the fact that the mind is *present in* the body. And will not this relation be either identical with that of ownership or involved in its analysis?

(E) Stout's theory I reject.[1] For I cannot accept his logical connexion between mental and bodily events founded upon the *completing* by the one of the other.

(F) A modification of Stout's theory and interactionism seems to me not unplausible. Suppose that consciousness is in fact spread throughout a body: let us take literally the expressions "I felt a pain in my finger" and "My mind is present in my body". Let us further suppose that bodily and mental events occasion each other. Then might we not claim that *co-presence* and *co-occasioning* constitute *ownership*. "*M* owns *B*" would mean, "The mental events which make up *M* and the material events which make up *B* occupy the same space and occasion each other".

I am very far from clear as to what is meant by consciousness occupying the area of my body. Consciousness is not an extensive quality; it does not occupy space in the same sense as red does. And we must remember that I may be conscious of distant objects. But perhaps *power of consciousness* occupies the area of my body in the way that electrical and magnetic powers occupy the area of my body.

[1] Or rather 'cannot at present see to be true'.

CHAPTER VIII

FREEWILL

1. **Freewill and Causation.** The problem of the freedom of the will arises, like so many philosophical problems, from an apparent contradiction between two beliefs which both seem well justified. We believe that everything which happens is due to something else which caused it to happen. This is the belief in the Law of Causation. We also believe that, when we decide to do one thing rather than another, then we are free to do otherwise. For example, you were free to get up five minutes earlier this morning. This is the belief in Freewill. Now by the Law of Causation your decision to act as you did was due to something which happened before, that is, it was caused and determined by what had gone before. But, if that is so, how can we say that you were free to have acted otherwise?

This argument may not impress you very much. You may say, "The argument which you have just stated is expressed in very vague language; so much so that I suspect that it does not prove that the Law of Causation and the Doctrine of Freewill are incompatible. And, on the other hand, I feel very sure that the Law of Causation is true and also that the Doctrine of Freewill is true. Now if they are both true, they cannot be incompatible".

True. At the same time, one would like to be able to see *what* is the matter with the argument criticised in this rather cavalier manner and to be able to remove the uncomfortable feeling of muddle which arises because of the apparent contradiction which it presents.

By an *apparent* contradiction is meant a *verbal* contradiction. By a *real* contradiction is meant a difference of opinion, a contradiction between what two people believe. There is a verbal contradiction when one person says, "So and so is such and such", and another person says, "It is not true that so and so is such and such". Thus suppose I say, "Guildford is 33 miles from London", and you say, "It is not true that Guildford is 33 miles from London", or say something which looks as if it entails that Guildford is not 33 miles from London, such as, "Guildford is 38 miles from London": in each case there is a verbal contradiction. But suppose it turns out that I meant by 'miles' statute miles and you meant by 'miles' geographical miles, then although you verbally contradicted me, you did not 'really' do so; in other words, what you meant was not incompatible with what I meant. There was *verbal* contradiction because the words you used might have led your hearers to imagine that what you meant, that is, what you believed, was incompatible with what I believed. But there was no 'real' contradiction; because what you in fact believed was not incompatible with what I believed.

Sometimes, of course, verbal contradiction is accompanied by real contradiction. Suppose you and I are watching a race and you say, "He'll win", and I say, "He won't", and we are both referring to the same horse, then I really contradict you.

Sometimes it is very difficult to tell whether a verbal contradiction is merely verbal or not. If the words

which you and I use are well known to have many different meanings, then a verbal contradiction between us
will probably be merely verbal. But when it is very
difficult to see how the words which you use could have
a different meaning from those which I use, then one
suspects a "real difference of opinion".

"Every event is determined" and "Some events,
namely decisions, are not determined" have been
thought by some philosophers to present a real contradiction. This is partly because some philosophers have
been rather frivolous or pugnacious and apt to suppose
that verbal contradictions are real contradictions in order
to start a fight. So, instead of trying to see what their
opponents could have meant, they have assumed that
their opponents were contradicting them, and have then
busied themselves in defending their own statements.

Thus people have thought it necessary to defend the
Law of Causation against the sentimental and intellectu-
ally irreverent supporters of Freewill by pointing out
that "all modern science is based on" this law. This
argument is a little curious. For if modern science is
based on the Law of Causation how can we base the Law
of Causation on it? I think this objection could be met.
But I propose not to bother about the point. For it
seems to me that the Law of Causation is quite capable
of looking after itself. I do not know *how* we know that
things are as they are because things were as they were.
But we do know it. The exact size of each iceberg in the
Antarctic is exactly fixed by its size a moment ago and
the wind and weather then prevailing; and these things
are fixed in their turn by preceding conditions. Hence

the exact size of each iceberg in the Antarctic is fixed by
the icebergs and the weather of a million years ago.

Again, people have defended, with almost pathetic
earnestness, the view that when they sinned they were
free to do differently. They have argued, quite rightly,
that if they had not been free to do otherwise, then what
they did would not have been sin.

Thus this pugnacious spirit has left us with the contradiction more firmly set than ever. But quite apart
from pugnacity it is extremely difficult to see any sense
of "Our decisions are not completely determined"
which is not incompatible with what is meant by "Every
event is determined".

A verbal contradiction can be 'removed' in two ways.
(*a*) If it is also real then the less well-established of the
conflicting opinions must be given up. (*b*) If it is not
real, the non-contradictory opinions expressed by the
contradictory words must be set out. The first method,
as we have seen, has been applied in the Causation-Free-
will contradiction without success. For both the Doctrine of Freewill and the Law of Causation seem equally
undeniable. As usual, it is the second method which
must be applied.

But now a difficulty arises. Suppose we find *a* sense
of Freewill compatible with the Law of Causation—
would that be enough? Certainly not. We want to be
sure with regard to *every* sense, in which it can be
plausibly claimed thàt we have Freewill, that it is compatible with the Law of Causation. Now there is one sense
of Freewill which it is very hard to reconcile with the
Law of Causation. This is why even serious philoso

phers, who have tried to reconcile the two, have been reluctantly compelled to give up the attempt and quell the disturbance by slaughtering one of the combatants. This sense of Freewill is really the only one which need give any trouble. It is the sense of Freewill which is implied by Blame.[1]

2. **Blame entails Freewill.** If anyone has ever done something for which he is to blame, then he has been free to do differently. Suppose that a man is on trial for not having prevented the murder of his cook. It is suggested that he is to blame for not having thrown out the murderer. Directly it is shown that he was physically incapable of doing so, the suggestion is withdrawn; though of course it would still be held that he ought to have thrown out the murderer *if* he could. It is next suggested that he is to blame for not telephoning to the police. But directly it is shown that he did not know how to use a telephone it is no longer held that he is to blame for not telephoning. It may, indeed, be thought that "he ought to have known at his age"; but that is to accuse him of a different crime; for it is to accuse him of carelessness in the past, not callousness in the present. In general then: You cannot be to blame for not doing what you were not able or free to do, and you cannot be to blame for doing what you could not avoid. This has

[1] There is a peculiar metaphysical use of 'free' in which a man is said to act freely when he acts 'in accordance with the dictates of his true self'. This is a misleading use of 'true' and means 'in accordance with his best desires'. In this sense no man acts freely when he acts culpably. This sort of freedom is quite compatible with the Law of Causation.

been expressed briefly by saying that *Ought* implies *Can*; and we will express it by saying that *Blame* entails *Free-will*. But in what sense?

3. In what sense?

3.1. BLAME ENTAILS FREEDOM OF SELF-DETERMINA-TION. Unless our behaviour is partly determined by our nature, we are never to blame. Unless it is true that with a different nature I should have behaved differently, I cannot be to blame for anything I have done. But this is not enough.

3.2. BLAME ENTAILS MORE THAN FREEDOM OF SELF-DETERMINATION. For watches and motor-cars have freedom of self-determination. A good watch keeps good time in spite of vibration, but a bad one does not; the behaviour of your car on steep hills would be different if its gear ratios were different. And we do not blame ourselves for reflex acts, such as uncontrollable coughing. Yet these are due to our nature. We blame ourselves only for willed acts, i.e. actions which are due to decision or desire.[1] The more deliberate a wrong act, the more to blame is the agent.

3.3. BLAME ENTAILS FREEDOM OF SELF-DIRECTION. We are not to blame for an act unless we could have done differently if we had wanted to. We are not to blame for failing to do an act unless we could have done it, i.e. we are not to blame unless it was open to us to do it, in the sense that we should have done it if we had decided to do

[1] For analysis of decision see p. 41.

it. Watches cannot make decisions. Therefore they lack free*will* or freedom of self-direction.

Freedom of self-direction is necessary for blame. It has been claimed that it is sufficient. It has been suggested that to blame a man for an act is to say that he did it from an evil motive; that to blame a man for speaking so as to hurt someone's feelings is just to say that his decision to speak so was due to evil intentions.[1] This suggestion is extremely plausible. It explains why we can blame only conscious things and why we can blame these only when the harm they do is intentional. But it has also been claimed that this freedom of self-direction is not enough. Let us examine this claim.

3.4. BLAME ENTAILS MORE THAN FREEDOM OF SELF-DIRECTION. Suppose that all your acts are determined by your decisions, and your decisions by your knowledge (no doubt imperfect) of the consequences of your acts together with your desires for these consequences. But suppose that on the occasion of each decision the strength of your various desires is fixed by the Devil. Suppose that you float a bogus company and ruin thousands. Are you to blame? I believe that you are not. It is a question for inspection. I have confirmed what I seem to see from inspection by asking others to inspect the same problem. I have carefully asked this question of more than one person who was highly intelligent but sufficiently ignorant of philosophy to have no axe to grind, and have received the reply that in such a case you would not be to blame. And I have asked at

[1] McTaggart, *Some Dogmas of Religion*, Chap. v, Sect. 127.

least two, and I think three, groups of about eighty students this same question, and a large majority favour the answer that in such a case you would not be to blame.[1]

Yet in this case your act was due to your nature—you had freedom of self-determination. Further your act was due to that part of your nature which is called your will—you had freedom of self-direction.

Before deciding this question take one more case. Suppose again that your acts are determined by your decisions, and your decisions by your wishes, and your wishes by the possibilities which your environment presents to you together with your disposition on which that environment acts. Suppose that your disposition is determined by the nature of your parents, and the nature of your parents by the natures of Adam and Eve. Suppose that the natures of Adam and Eve were determined by God. In such a case are you rightly blamed for your acts? You are responsible for them but is it not God who is *ultimately* responsible for them?[2]

I think that here again, in this example, which does not differ in principle from the first, we must agree with those who say that you are not to blame.

And that this is the right answer is now confirmed by our being able to see *why* you are not to blame. You are not to blame because, although responsible for your acts, you are not *ultimately* responsible for them.

[1] I propose to obtain exact figures later.
[2] "Thou wilt not with Predestination round enmesh me, and impute my Fall to Sin." Omar Khayyam, *Rubaiyat*.

3.5. BLAME ENTAILS NOT ONLY SELF-DIRECTION BUT ULTIMATE SELF-DIRECTION. You can, then, be blamed for an act only in so far as that act is caused by your nature, and, in particular, by your will; further, your will must be at least part of the *ultimate* cause of your act. To say that your will is part of the ultimate cause of your act is to say that while your will determines your act that will is not in its turn completely determined by something which is not your will. What blame requires is that, however far back we go in setting out the causes of your act, we shall never come to a time at which a set of purely external circumstances, i.e. not involving you and your will, formed a complete cause of your act.[1] Therefore, if you are to blame for an act *A*, then either (α) at some time the series of causes of your decision to do *A* becomes incomplete or ceases altogether, or (β) the series is an infinite series of determinations of your will by your will.

4. **Compatibility of ultimate Self-direction with the Law of Causation.** Let us consider a typical decision and act: you decide to take cocaine and take it. You realise the danger you run of ill-health for yourself, and thus of injury to your friends. You are to blame for this act. Hence as we have seen that act must be ultimately due to your will.

[1] The expression "the complete cause of *X*" is ambiguous. It may mean "all the events *of a given period* which made up a complete cause of *X*" and it may mean "all the sets of events in the chain of sets of events which caused *X*". *A* complete cause of an act is a set of events *of a given period* which sufficed completely to determine the occurrence of that act.

It looks as if alternative (α) above, according to which you are ultimately responsible in that your decision or one of its direct or indirect causes is wholly or partially undetermined, is incompatible with the Law of Causation. There are, however, two ways in which it might be suggested that even Indeterminism can be reconciled with the Law of Causation.

4.1. DETERMINATION BY DISPOSITION. (i) Your act in taking cocaine was due in part to your disposition. For your act was due to your decision, and your decision to your desires, and your desires were due in part to your environment (your packet of cocaine) and in part to your disposition which that environment acted upon. (ii) Your disposition is an undetermined fact. (iii) This is not incompatible with the Law of Causation. For the Law of Causation states that every *event* has a cause. Now your disposition is not an event, and it is not even a complete particular fact equivalent to an event. For your disposition is made up, not of *actual* thoughts and feelings, but of *tendencies* to feel in such and such a way whenever you are stimulated in such and such a way. For example, to say that you are irritable is to say that *if* anyone thwarts you at all *then* you will strongly desire to injure him.

It must be admitted that these 'if-then' facts, which make up one's disposition, are not events nor equivalent to events. They do not state that anything *is* occurring. They state what event *would* occur if such and such another event took place. And these 'if-then' facts about individuals may well be ultimate, just as the most general physical properties of particles are ultimate. No one explains the fact that particles react to stimuli in accordance with the laws of motion.

Now it must be admitted that we do in some sense 'explain' the fact that *you* accepted cocaine while *I* refused it, by saying that you are of a rash disposition while I am cautious, that is, by a difference in our properties.

But is this explanation in the sense of *giving the cause of* the difference in our reactions? Is it not merely to bring the particular case of the reaction to cocaine and neglect of its dangers under a general heading—*another* instance of your neglecting danger?

When I explain the fact that *my* watch stops when I ride a motor-cycle while *your* watch keeps going, by saying that my watch stops from vibration, then I explain only in the sense of bringing the motor-cycle case under a general heading. But the cause of the difference in reaction is not given until there is found that difference of structure (actual condition) between the two watches which caused the difference in reaction. This explanation will again involve properties, but the final explanation will involve only properties which apply to *all* material things, and there will then remain no cases of different reaction to the same stimulus. Thus in physics and chemistry it is assumed that for every difference of property there is a difference in structure, and that the only causes of difference in reaction are differences in structure, i.e. the actual state, i.e. the qualities and relations of the particles involved, as opposed to 'if-then' facts about them.

Perhaps persons are different. Perhaps differences in the properties or dispositions of persons are not reducible to differences in actual state. It may be that there are differences, at least in degree or strength, between the *ultimate* dispositions or properties of one person and those of another. If so, these differences in degree between your dispositions and mine will be part of the cause of the differences in our reactions. If this is possible, we may welcome this suggestion as supplementary to the suggestion of the long series of determinations of decision and desires by preceding decisions and desires which we shall have to consider later.

But *is* it sense to say that part of the cause of your strong desire for cocaine now is the fact that, if and when you are offered cocaine, then you strongly desire it? Again, *is* it sense to say that part of the cause of your disregard for this danger is the fact that you always disregard any danger? This question is enough to show that the disposition theory is, on the face of it, unsatisfactory.

It may be answered that, even if differences in property are not ultimate, their ultimacy can be avoided only by supposing corresponding 'structural' differences—differences in the actual state of people with different properties. That is so. But then must the 'structural' differences be differences in *mental* condition, for example, prevailing mood? May they not be quite literally structural differences in the nervous system, etc.? Perhaps the irritable man is irritable wholly because of his digestion.

It is impossible to carry this discussion further here. In any case the suggestion of Determination by Disposition would, I think, supplement rather than supplant the possibilities of reconciliation which we shall next consider.

4.2. THE FINITE SERIES OF INTERNAL DETERMINA-TIONS. There is another way in which alternative (α) (p. 118), according to which one of the causes direct or indirect of your decision was partially or wholly undetermined, is reconcilable with the Law of Causation in a mild form.

The Law of Causation in a mild form is not incompatible with a First Cause. The Law of Causation in a mild form is not the law that *every* event has a cause but is the law that all events, *except those which occurred first in order of time*, have causes. So that we might suppose that, if we trace back the causes of your decision, we shall find, not indeed an endless series of determinations of your will by your will, but a world-long series which ended not at your birth but at the beginning of time amongst the events which were the first causes.

It must, however, be clearly understood that the series shall not end or become incomplete[1] until the first causes are reached. Anything else is incompatible with even the mild form of the Law of Causation. There cannot be decisions now which are incompletely determined in that their direct causes are incomplete.

[1] The series cannot become incomplete, as opposed to ending. For let E be an event which is incompletely but partially determined. Then since it is partially determined, it must have been preceded by an event which partially determined it. But if it is preceded by an event, it cannot be among the first causes. Therefore it must be completely determined.

4.3. THE INFINITE SERIES OF INTERNAL DETERMINA-
TIONS. If one set of events, namely the first, is not determined, it is difficult to see how we know that all the rest
are. This suggests that we know the stronger form of the
Law of Causation according to which *every* event is
completely determined.

This form of the Law of Causation is not reconcilable
with the finite, though world-long, series of internal
determinations. It requires alternative (β) according to
which every decision is determined by an infinite series
of internal determinations. This alternative, of course,
is compatible with the strict form of the Law of Causation; and, since the determinations which it contem-
plates are all of the will by the will, it is compatible with
ultimate self-direction and blame.

4.4. THE SERIES OF INTERNAL DETERMINATIONS MUST
BE EITHER INFINITE OR WORLD-LONG. It appears then
that if (i) either form of the Law of Causation is true,
and (ii) we are to blame for our acts, then each decision is due to an either infinite or world-long series of
determinations of the will by the will. We shall find that
this consequence, so far from being incredible, is merely
surprising to the western world. For there is no good
reason against it, and we shall see in a moment that it is
what we might have expected on independent grounds.

4.5. INDEPENDENT SUPPORT OF THIS CONCLUSION.
When you decide to take cocaine, your decision is caused
by the ratio of your strong desire for its taste to your
feeble desire to avoid its dangers; and your desires are
caused partly by something in your environment—you

see your packet of cocaine—but also partly by your past decisions to take cocaine. For your present strong desire is acquired and thus due to past decisions to take cocaine. Of course, when you were first offered cocaine, your decision to take it cannot have been determined by past decisions to take cocaine. Nevertheless, it was probably in part determined by past decisions. For it was in part due, as we say, to your character at the time that the cocaine was first offered to you. And is not your character at any given time, in part at least, determined by what you have done in the past?

"But", you will say, "what about the first decision I made after I was born? That cannot have been in part determined by other decisions of mine."

But was it your first decision? We are too ignorant of what happens at birth to have any good reason from experience for asserting that the first decision which you made after birth was your first decision. Nor is there any good philosophical reason for this assertion.

On the contrary, we have a reason independent of the argument from responsibility in favour of supposing that it was not your first decision, or at least that it was preceded by the manifestation of will in desire. Let us suppose, for the sake of simplicity, that the first mental event at birth was a decision. By the principle of continuity we know that a mental event and therefore a decision is not completely explained by purely material circumstances (see p. 95). The decision therefore was partly caused by and therefore preceded by a non-material event.

We know of no non-material events which are not

mental. Further, by the principle of the resemblance of the cause this non-material event must at least contain a mental event.

Now I submit that the most probable hypothesis as to the nature of that mental event which contributed to your decision is that (*a*) it was a mental event in *your* mind, and (*b*) involved your *will*. For without (*a*) we have to suppose the *direct* action of one mind on another —a thing which rarely if ever happens. And, as for (*b*), if a decision has a mental explanation at all, it is always in terms of desires; and, if desires have a mental explanation at all, it is always in terms of other desires[1] (see p. 89).

So far then from its being incredible that your decision at birth should be not the first manifestation of your will but determined by previous manifestations, this is what we might have expected quite apart from any argument from ultimate responsibility.

What the argument from blame and ultimate self-direction does, is to confirm the conclusion that a decision (i) cannot have purely material causes, (ii) has a cause which (*a*) is mental, (*b*) is an event in the history of the mind which makes the decision, and

---

[1] The principle of the resemblance of the cause is probably at work here. For though we have said that *is wishing* and *is cognizing* are species of *is conscious*, it may well be that they are both in a sense supreme variables related to *is conscious* as *has an extensive quality* and *has a spatial character* are related to *is material*. Extensive quality and spatial character are aspects of materiality, each of which implies the other though neither is explainable by the other.

(*c*) is concerned with that mind's will, that is, its desires or decisions.

From the Law of Causation it follows that this second voluntary event has in its turn a cause. This cause by another application of the argument from the principles of continuity and ultimate responsibility must again be a voluntary event in the history of the same mind.

This process continues indefinitely or until the first causes are reached.

The argument from responsibility is particularly important for the following reason. It proves that the mental event, which by the principle of the resemblance of the cause must precede any mental event in the mind of *X*, must be a mental event *in the mind of X* and not in the mind of God or some 'general consciousness'.

5. Freedom of Indeterminism. You will have noticed that we have refused to accept freedom of indeterminism, that is, the doctrine that our decisions are not completely determined by our desires or else our desires are not completely determined by our environment, character and preceding mental state. We refused to accept this view because it conflicts with the Law of Causation. Most of those who have accepted indeterminism have done so, I think, because they mistakenly supposed that blame requires it. But other reasons have been advanced and we must consider them, especially as freedom of indeterminism would save us from pre-existence.

(i) *Inspection.* It has been urged, in the first place,

that in the case of some of our decisions we can see by inspection that they are not completely determined.

This is a surprising contention. We must admit, at once, that there are a great many facts about the causation of our decisions which we can learn by inspection. But all these facts are *positive* like the fact *I decided to go because I hated him*. How can I know by inspection the *negative* fact that my decision is not completely determined?

I believe that people have maintained that they do know that their decisions are not completely determined because of one of two confusions. First they confuse this freedom of indeterminism with freedom of self-direction. I *can* tell by inspection (roughly speaking) that I could have done otherwise *if I would*. But this is merely to say that different causes, namely different desires, would have caused a different result, namely different decision and action. This is quite consistent with the Law of Causation. But then it is not indeterminism.

Secondly, people have confused the claim that they know directly that their decisions are not completely determined, with the claim that this can be *proved* by the argument from Action in the Line of Greatest Resistance. Let us consider this argument.

(ii) *Action in the Line of Greatest Resistance.* It is asserted that we sometimes do an act *A* instead of an act *A'* even when our discoverable motives for *A* are weaker than our discoverable motives for *A'*. Thus sometimes we go to a concert instead of a cinema even when we really have the feeblest interest in music and are very fond of the cinema. We feel we *ought* to go to the concert. This ethical motive reinforces our feeble desire for the music. Even so, it is incredible that the watery ethical desire and the feeble musical desire should counterbalance the strong desire to see Owen Nares or Anna May Wong. Therefore, it is concluded, our decision is not completely determined by our desires and therefore not completely determined at all. Again, we sometimes treat people unkindly when we are very fond of them; and we sometimes do this continually, even when we are not suffering from liver or some other temporary disturbance. And we sometimes make great efforts to see someone who is 'nothing to us'. From this again it is concluded that our decisions and acts are not completely determined by our desires and are therefore not completely determined.

The concert case differs from the other two, and in replying to these arguments I propose to take it first.

It seems to me that McDougall[1] has dealt with this case. It is plausible to say that the discoverable motives for the concert are feebler than those for the cinema, only if a certain motive for the concert, of great importance but of a peculiar kind, is ignored. This is the desire to be an admirable person in being a lover of music; in other words, one desires to desire the concert because one anticipates admiration from oneself and one's fellows if only one can 'adore music'. It is this secondary desire—a desire for a desire—which, though

[1] *Introduction to Social Psychology*, p. 198. McDougall does *not* explain why we admire a person who, for example, adores music.

128

of this peculiar kind, is very strong and quite able to drive one to the concert.

The other cases are different. One does not admire oneself for making great efforts to see X, nor does one expect others to admire one for making these efforts. Much less does one admire oneself for being unkind to a friend. Indeed we must admit that in such cases we can sometimes be sure that the observable motives were not the complete cause of the decision. But how do we know that there is not some other motive which is unobservable and which yet affects one's decision and one's acts? We cannot know this unless we assume that every desire affecting decision can be detected by introspection. And no one will maintain this; especially in view of the evidence which the psycho-analysts provide for motives undiscoverable by introspection.

6. **Summary.** We found that the fact that a person is to blame for an act entails, not merely self-determination and not merely self-direction, but ultimate self-direction. In other words, however far back we trace the causes of a culprit's conduct, we must never reach a set of causes which were the complete cause of his conduct but were none of them concerned with him and his will. Therefore either (α) at some time the series of causes of his act ceases or becomes incomplete, or (β) for ever the complete cause of his conduct will concern in some degree him and his will.

The indeterminist accepts (α) and tries to support his position by an argument from action in the line of greatest resistance. But this argument is unsound. And we reject (α) unless it is admitted that the series of complete causes, each involving the culprit's will, does not cease until the beginning of time among the first causes. With so much admitted, this alternative is not incompatible with the mild form of the Law of Causation, according to which all events are completely determined except those which occurred first in order of time. It is, however, incompatible with the more plausible form of the Law of Causation, according to which *every* event is determined. In this form the Law of Causation can be reconciled with ultimate responsibility[1] only by supposing that the series of determinations of the will by the will is endless.

Therefore, in any case, the series of determinations of X's will by X's will must be at least world-long.

This conclusion is independently supported by the principles of continuity and resemblance.

Pre-existence then follows from our considerations in this Part of the book.[2] This pre-existence must have been world-long.[3] It may or may not have been of a very feeble kind.[4]

---

[1] The considerations in this chapter suggest that the usual judgments of blame are considerably exaggerated.

[2] It is hardly necessary to warn the reader that this sort of conclusion is unfashionable.

[3] If every event is determined then there is no finite period such that the totality of determinations did not occupy a longer period. This does not follow from the fact that the number of determinations is infinite, but from the fact that any set of events, the earlier of which determine the later, is itself an event.

[4] Compare Dr Broad's theory of a psychical factor. The psychical factor would not serve unless it were at least feeble consciousness. *The Mind and Its Place in Nature*, p. 535.

FURTHER READING

For a somewhat fuller account of the nervous system and the correlations between body and mind see Collins and Drever, *Experimental Psychology*.

* The relation between body and mind is distinguished by Broad on pp. 95 and 96 of *The Mind and Its Place in Nature*. Materialism he refutes in Chap. xiv. In Chap. iii he discusses at "the level of enlightened common sense" the causal connexion between body and mind.

This last topic receives more difficult but more fundamental treatment in Stout's *Mind and Matter*, Book iii.

On the freedom of the will see McTaggart, *Some Dogmas of Religion*; Moore, *Ethics*; Broad, *Determinism, Indeterminism and Libertarianism*. This last is closely connected with the above, but was published after I had written this book.

PART II

Cognition

CHAPTER IX

PERCEPTION

1. **Normal Perception.** We come now to the second of those relations between body and mind, which we hoped to analyse, namely what we have called knowledge or cognition. 'Knowledge' is equivalent to cognition only when the word 'knowledge' is used in a very broad sense for any species of consciousness in which something is present to the mind. For perceptions and sensations and the 'sensations' and beliefs of dreams, as well as ordinary knowledge of truths, are included under cognition. Let us begin with perception, and, in particular, with vision.

We are concerned then with what may be called a normal visual perception. By a 'visual perception' I mean such a fact as is expressed by "I see a penny", "I see a chair", "I see a cat". By 'normal' I wish to exclude cases in which I see a penny through coloured spectacles or half-immersed in water, or under a microscope, or in a mirror, or double. We may find that these abnormal perceptions help us to analyse the normal perceptions, but we shall consider them only in so far as they throw light upon the analysis of normal perceptions.

The definition of 'visual perception' which has been offered suffers from a serious ambiguity because "I see a penny" is ambiguous. Suppose you go out into the dusk to look for Jones. You pass two men in a lane and subsequently learn that one was Jones, although it was so dark when you passed them that you did not know that one of them was Jones. On your return, Smith asks you, "Did you see Jones?" If you reply, "No", you may mislead Smith; for you saw something which in fact was Jones. And if you reply, "Yes", again you may mislead Smith; for he may think from your answer that you not merely saw something which in fact was Jones, but also knew that that something was Jones. In general, "Y sees a penny" may mean "Y sees something which is in fact a penny", and it may mean "Y sees something which is in fact a penny and believes it is a penny". It will be seen that both kinds of perception contain a sensation, i.e. a sensing of something as having a sense-quality,[1] and a relationship between what is sensed and a material thing. We will concern ourselves with the first and more fundamental sense of 'seeing'. This is the sense of 'see' in which I can be said to have seen Jones even when I mistook him for his brother.[2]

2. **The Problem.** We are not concerned with the question, "Do pennies and chairs exist?" This question would be worth asking only if we knew something with greater certainty than we know that there is a chair in this room. Now of course philosophers have

---

[1] For definition of 'sensation' see p. 41.

[2] I am not using 'see' in the unconventional way in which some philosophers have found it useful to use it. In this unconventional sense of the word it is correct to say "I see a pink rat", even when there is no pink rat for me to see.

attached meanings to such expressions as "There is a chair in this room" which would make it doubtful whether it expresses a fact. We, on the other hand, are not starting with the assumption that "There is a chair in this room" means so and so and yet expresses a fact. We are starting with the assumption that "There is a chair in this room" in its ordinary meaning *whatever that may be*, sometimes expresses a fact. We assume too that "I see a penny", as usually used, sometimes expresses a fact. And we want to know what the fundamental elements of that fact are and how they are arranged; we want to know its constituents, the components which relate the constituents, and the order of this relating.

If we were to take the sentences, "I saw Jones", "I see a penny", as guides to the analysis of the facts they express, we should say that each of these facts is two-termed, and that the constituents of the first are Jones and I, while the constituents of the second are a particular penny and I, and that the component of each fact is the relation *seeing*.

This would be all very well as far as it went. *I saw Jones* is two-termed in the sense in which *I prefer Jones to Smith* is three-termed, and in this sense of 'term' Jones and I are the two terms, i.e. constituents. But if we look more closely we shall see that the situations are a good deal more complex than the sentences suggest,[1] and in some more fundamental sense of 'term' contain a great many more than two terms or constituents. What is wanted is a list of the most fundamental

[1] See Broad, *The Mind and Its Place in Nature*, p. 141.

constituents of the situation, together with a clear indication of how they are related. This, unfortunately, I am not able to give; and so I am obliged to give a list of constituents which very likely mixes fundamental with non-fundamental constituents in a pretty scandalous way.

The only way in which we can gain a clearer apprehension of the fundamental structure of the fact expressed by "I see a penny" is to translate the sentence "I see a penny" into a sentence which shall more clearly reveal this fundamental structure. If one sentence is a translation of another then the one expresses exactly what the other does, and therefore when the one is true the other is. Hence our translation of "I see a penny" must be true whenever "I see a penny" is true and never otherwise.[1] Consequently we are able to set down certain conditions which any translation of "I see a penny" must fulfil; and these conditions will help us, when a translation is suggested, to decide whether it will do.

3. **The Conditions of Correct Analysis of Perception.** The analysis must permit that:

I. Sometimes you and I see the same part of the same penny. For example, if a penny is lying 'tails' up on a table in front of us, then we can both see the 'tails' side of the penny. This is sometimes expressed by saying that pennies, chairs and tables are *public* objects.

II. Sometimes I see and touch the same penny. This

[1] For a fuller explanation of this point see p. 186.

is sometimes expressed by saying that the penny is *neutral between different senses*.

III. Sometimes I can be sure that a penny has not changed in shape or size or colour or temperature, from what it was a minute ago, even though it now looks a different shape, or size, or colour, or feels a different temperature. For example, on the horizon the moon looks bigger than it does when it is high in the sky though it is not really any bigger. And, when your hands are warm, the hand of someone else will not feel warm to you; but, if you put your hands in ice, then afterwards his hand will feel very warm to you though its temperature has not changed. This is sometimes expressed by saying that the penny is *independent* of its observer. This is not a very good way of putting this condition because it suggests that no changes in the observer make any difference to the penny. Yet it may be that every change in the observer makes *some* change in the penny. The point is that a certain kind of change in the observer, namely a change from first seeing the penny as having one character to then seeing the penny as having another character, does not always produce a certain kind of change in the object, namely a change from first having the one character to then having the other.

We may next proceed to the analysis of *I see a penny*. What is wanted, we must remember, is a list of the most fundamental constituents of that fact, together with a clear indication of how they are related.

4. **The Constituents of Perception.** The following

is a list of things which are in some sense constituents of normal visual perceptions:

(i) The Observer.
(ii) The Material Object.
(iii) The Observed Side of the Object.
(iv) The Corresponding Sense-datum.
(v) The Sense-qualities.

Thus, when I am looking at a penny which lies 'tails' side up, then (1) I am the observer, (2) the penny is the object, (3) the 'tails' but not the 'heads' side of the penny is *the observed side* of the penny, (4) something which seems brown and elliptical to me is the *corresponding sense-datum*, (5) browness and ellipticity are the *sense-qualities*. The last three expressions require further explanation.

4.1. THE OBSERVED SIDE OF THE OBJECT. When I see an object, such as a penny or a table, there are many of its parts which I cannot see; on the other hand, there are parts of it which I can see. The part that I see when I look at an object is what I am calling the "observed side or surface of the object". For example, I may fully see the 'tails' side of a penny or the top of a table, while unable to see the 'heads' side of the penny, or the legs of the table. Indeed, to see an object (as opposed to a surface) is partially to see it by fully seeing part of its surface. Of course, when I see an object there are ever so many parts of its surface which I can fully see. But only one of these is the *whole* of what I can fully see. That part of the surface of an object which is the whole of that much of its surface which I can fully see, I call the *observed surface* of the object.

Two points should be noticed. (*a*) It is quite proper and good conventional English to say that one sees an object such as a penny or a house, even when one is fully seeing only a part (say the front-door part) of its surface. And it is also good English to say, "No, I could not see the back of the house, only the front side". There are therefore two senses of 'seeing'. The one is applicable to objects, and is the sense which we distinguished above as the one to be analysed. The second sense of 'seeing' is applicable to surfaces. It looks as if the sense applicable to objects is analysable in terms of that applicable to surfaces. (*b*) A surface or side of an object is not a part of the object in the plain sense in which my thumb is part of my hand, but only in the sense in which the *surface* of my thumb is part of the *surface* of my hand.

4.2. SENSE-QUALITIES. Colours, sounds, temperatures, smells, tastes, roughness, smoothness, sizes and shapes and distances, are characters apprehended by the senses. They are sense-characters. As we have seen, they are quite unlike such qualities[1] as happy, loves, and loathes, which are psychological or personal qualities. Personal qualities are apprehended only by introspecting them in ourselves; we infer their presence in others from their talk, smiles, and grimaces. Sense-qualities are apprehended in sensation (for definition

[1] It is usual to speak of sense-qualities, although we must include sense-relations, such as distance.

of sensation see p. 41). It is important to reconsider here the examples there provided.

4.3. SENSE-DATA. You and I have personal qualities and so we are called 'persons'. Of course you are not the same thing as kindness or happiness; you are not identical with your qualities, but you are said to possess or be characterised by these qualities. Persons, then, are the things which possess personal qualities. And sense-data are not identical with sense-qualities but are the things which possess *or* seem to possess sense-qualities.

Two difficulties present themselves. Are not pennies brown, smooth and cool, and are not dogs' tongues pink, rough and warm? Yet surely they are not sense-data? The answer here is easy.[1] Pennies *are* brown, but only in the sense that their surfaces are brown. A penny or cake is rightly called brown even when it is yellow inside. Thus surfaces are brown in a more fundamental sense[2] than are the objects of which they are the surfaces. Likewise, sense-data are brown in a more fundamental sense than are objects.

"But", it may be said, "are they brown in any sense more fundamental than that in which the *surfaces* of objects are brown? And, if not, why have you introduced the new and troublesome expression 'sense-datum' when the familiar expression 'surface of an object' would have served?"

The answer here is as follows: If we confine ourselves to visual sense-data, it is true that they are all

[1] It is superficially easy.
[2] For definition of 'more fundamental' see p. 13.

surfaces in the sense of being two-dimensional. But is it certain that they are surfaces *of something*? In your dreams you see expanses of blue, and these are surfaces in the sense that they are two-dimensional. But of what are they the surfaces? Again, suppose you obtain an after-image in the form of a red patch, after looking at a piece of green paper on a grey wall.[1] This red patch is two-dimensional, but is it part of the surface of the wall? Perhaps it is; perhaps we know it is. But many people have denied this, and it is part of our enquiry to decide whether they were right. Consequently we must avoid framing our definition so as to beg this question. Hence, although sense-data may in fact possess sense-qualities in the very sense in which the surfaces of pennies and dogs' tongues possess them, and may be identical with these surfaces, we must not *define* them as these surfaces. We will define them as what possess and/or are sensed as possessing sense-qualities in the most fundamental sense of 'possess' and 'sensed as possessing'. If these fundamental senses of 'possess' and 'sensed as possessing' turn out to be identical with those applicable to the surfaces of pennies and dogs' tongues, so much the better.

4.4. THE CORRESPONDING SENSE-DATUM.[2] Whenever you see an object, such as a penny, there is just one sense-datum which you are tempted to suppose is identical with the whole part which you can fully see

[1] See p. 42.

[2] This is not a completely accurate account of what Moore means by 'corresponding sense-datum'.

of the penny, that is with the observed surface of the penny. Even if this sense-datum is not identical with the observed surface, it certainly has *some* relation to that surface which it has to nothing else. We do not wish, at this stage, to decide whether this relation is that of identity with the observed surface, so we say that it *corresponds* to it.

5. The Relations between the Constituents of Perception. When I see a penny,

I. What is the relation of the corresponding sense-datum to the penny?

II. What is the analysis of the relation between (1) the corresponding sense-datum, (2) its sense-qualities (e.g. brownness and ellipticity), and (3) the observer (me)? This is the relation which we express by "I sense as brown and elliptical the corresponding sense-datum".

We shall find that these questions are not independent; that is, the answer to the one depends to some extent upon the answer to the other.

5.1. AS TO QUESTION I. The answer which at first seems plausible is:

(A) *The corresponding sense-datum is identical with the observed surface of the penny.* Owing to the difficulties to which this answer has led, many other answers have been suggested. I cannot put them all down here, but I mention three.

(B) *The corresponding sense-datum is an effect of the penny.* Thus it may be suggested that the penny is a number of electrons in violent motion and that the effect of these on a body or a mind or the combination of the two is a sense-datum sensed by that mind.

(C) *The relation between the corresponding sense-datum and the penny is unanalysable and it holds only between material objects and sense-data. It is a relation which each sense-datum has to only one object. We may express it by saying that the sense-datum is a 'manifestation of' the penny.*

(D) *Each object is a group or family of sense-data, all having a sort of family resemblance, all occupying a certain region of space, and all following one another according to regular rules.*[1] When I see a penny the corresponding sense-datum which I then sense is a member of the family of sense-data which is the penny.

I mention these views, not because I propose to discuss them all, but because I want to give an idea of the large number of possible answers to the question, "What relation holds between the sense-datum and the penny", and an idea of the sort of answers which have some plausibility.

5.2. AS TO QUESTION II. "Does the corresponding sense-datum really have the qualities which it is sensed as having, or does it merely appear to me to have these qualities?" This requires a little explanation. The relation expressed by "I sense this as brown" is certainly three-termed; because it involves (1) me, (2) the sense-quality, and (3) the sense-datum. But is it *ultimately*

---

[1] For the best working out of this view see H. H. Price, *Perception*.

three-termed, or is it a product of two two-termed relations? The relation expressed by "Albert is the paternal uncle of Charles" is three-termed, because it involves Albert and Charles and Charles' father. But it is not *ultimately* three-termed, because to say "Albert is the paternal uncle of Charles" is to say "(*a*) There is a man who is the father of Charles, and (*b*) that man is the brother of Albert". Thus the three-termed relation *paternal uncle* is resolvable into the two-termed relations *father of* and *brother of*. We cannot, however, resolve the three-termed fact *I sense this as brown* into two-termed facts, the one relating me to brownness and the other relating brownness to the sense-datum. Therefore *I sense this as brown* is an ultimately three-termed fact.

But some ultimately three-termed facts contain independent two-termed facts as parts, while others do not. The fact *I observed that Bob beat Bill* is three-termed and cannot be reduced to two-termed relationships. Nevertheless it contains the independent two-termed fact *Bob beat Bill*. The fact *Bob beat* Bill is *independent* in the sense that it might have been true that *Bob beat Bill* even if neither I nor anyone else had observed it. And this independent two-termed fact is contained in the fact *I observed that Bob beat Bill*. On the other hand, many three-termed facts do not contain any independent two-termed part. Thus, *I prefer Bob to Bill* does not contain any independent two-termed relationship between Bob and Bill. It might perhaps be thought that it contained the fact, *Bob is superior to Bill*. But reflexion shows at once that *I prefer*

Bob to Bill does not contain the fact that Bob is superior to Bill; for I might prefer Bob to Bill although Bill was superior to Bob. Again *I believe or judge that Bob is superior to Bill* does not contain an independent two-termed fact that Bob is superior to Bill. For my judgment may be false; and if it is false then either Bill is superior to Bob or neither is superior to the other, and each of these excludes *Bob is superior to Bill*. Hence, since my judgment can exist without the fact *Bob is superior to Bill*, my judgment cannot contain that fact.

Does *I sense this as brown* contain an independent two-termed fact *This is brown*? Is the fact *I sense this as brown* a species of observation? Or is *I sense this as brown* akin to a judgment, and thus a three-termed unity which does not contain a two-termed unity within itself?

This question may be put in another way. Some sentences which appear to be expressing one-termed facts are really expressing two-termed facts, and some which seem to be expressing two-termed facts are really expressing three-termed facts. Thus "Brown is kind" refers to some such two-termed fact as *Brown is kind to Jones*. Again "Brighton is preferable to Eastbourne" expresses the three-termed fact *Someone prefers Brighton to Eastbourne*. The two-termed sentence "Brighton is preferable to Eastbourne" is somewhat misleading, because it suggests that the fact it expresses is independent of the existence of anything besides Brighton and Eastbourne, while on writing out the sentence in a fuller form it appears at once that the fact it expresses involves the existence of something other than Brighton and Eastbourne, and further that this something is a mind. For nothing can prefer except something which is conscious. This is sometimes expressed by saying that the relation between Brighton and Eastbourne, which is expressed by "Brighton is preferable to Eastbourne" is *subjective*, i.e. is a relation which the one has to the other in virtue of an attitude which some mind takes up towards them.[1] Now, when we say of sense-data, "This is brown", "This is bigger than that", are these sentences misleading in a similar way? Do the facts which they express contain one more term than the sentences suggest, and is that term a mind? Are "This is brown", "This is hot", short for "This is sensed as brown by someone", "This is sensed as hot by someone"? and is "This is bigger than that" short for "This is sensed by someone as bigger than that?" If so, then the facts these sentences express are mind-dependent, and are not independent two-termed facts. On this view sense-facts, i.e. facts as to the sense-characters of sense-data, are *logically*, and not merely *causally*, mind-dependent. It is not merely that they come about because of minds, and thus *would* not exist without minds. They contain minds and a mental relation, namely *sensibly appearing*, and thus *could* not exist without minds.[2]

---

[1] The view that moral judgments are subjective leads to the definition—"*His motive is worse than mine*" means "*His motive would be more disliked by society than mine*".

[2] This, perhaps, is the view which Berkeley held.

It is now apparent that to ask "Does the corresponding sense-datum, when I see a penny, really have the qualities it is sensed as having, or does it merely appear to have them?" is not a very satisfactory way of putting our question. For we can certainly say of one patch that it is brown and of another that it is green. The question is as to what is *meant* by saying "This is brown". Does it express an independent, non-subjective, two-termed fact, or does it express a mind-dependent, subjective, three-termed fact? In other words, are 'brown', 'hot' and 'elliptical', as applied to sense-data, short for 'seems brown to someone', 'seems hot to someone' and 'seems elliptical to someone'. In short: "Are sense-qualities subjective?" We shall, however, often find it convenient to put this question in the form, "Do sense-data really have the qualities they are sensed as having or do they merely appear to have them?"

I now propose to prove an important connexion between one of the answers to question I and one of the answers to question II, which may be expressed thus:

5.3. EITHER (α) USUALLY THE CORRESPONDING SENSE-DATUM IS NOT THE SURFACE OR (β) USUALLY ITS QUALITIES ARE SUBJECTIVE. *When I see a penny then usually* either (α) *the corresponding sense-datum is not identical with the observed surface of the penny* or (β) *the corresponding sense-datum does not independently have the qualities which I sense it as having.*[1]

[1] *Usually either* (α) *or* (β) is equivalent to *Either usually* (α) *or usually* (β). For we may assume here that it is not sometimes (α) which is true and sometimes (β).

This is *not* equivalent to the statement: Usually *both* (α) the corresponding sense-datum is not identical with the observed surface of the penny *and* (β) the corresponding sense-datum does not independently have the qualities I sense it as having. It might seem unnecessary to point out such an obvious confusion, but scores of people have made it. On the other hand, the proposition *is* equivalent to the statement: Usually not both (α) and (β) are false, i.e., Usually not both (*a*) the corresponding sense-datum is the observed surface, and (*b*) the corresponding sense-datum independently has the qualities it appears to have.

To prove that usually (*a*) or (*b*) must go would be to prove something of importance. For (*a*) is a proposition which most people wish to assert when they begin to study the analysis of perception. It does seem to be the case when I see a penny that that which I sense as brown and elliptical is the observed surface of the penny. As Professor Moore says:[1] "I do now *seem* to be apprehending directly a part of the surface of my thumb...: from which, as I have said, it would seem to me to follow with practical certainty that the corresponding sense-datum is a part of the surface of my thumb...". And (*b*) is a proposition which few philosophers have doubted. When one looks at a red patch it seems as if there is *something* which is really red. Indeed, if either (*a*) or (*b*) is given up, it is not at all easy to see what we know about material things or how we know it. I shall mention two of the several proofs that (*a*) and (*b*) cannot both be true, i.e. that usually

[1] Aristotelian Society Supplementary Vol. ii, p. 185.

either (α) the corresponding sense-datum is not identical with the observed surface of the penny, or (β) the corresponding sense-datum does not really have the qualities it appears to have, i.e. that 'brown' means 'appears brown to me'. I shall begin by stating two general proofs that in many cases of an observer's seeing an object, either (α) the corresponding sense-datum is not identical with the observed surface of the object or (β) the corresponding sense-datum does not really have the qualities it is sensed as having. And I shall then illustrate this by stating the proof as applicable to the particular case in which I see a penny.

(i) The simpler proof may be stated as follows: Often when we see an object the corresponding sense-datum has qualities which are quite different from those which we know the observed surface to possess. In these cases then, either the corresponding sense-datum merely appears to have the qualities we sense or it is not identical with the observed surface. Thus we know that one surface of a penny is round. Yet when I see a penny the corresponding sense-datum which I then sense usually seems elliptical. When this is so either the corresponding sense-datum is not identical with the observed surface of the penny, or, although it *seems* elliptical, it is not really so.

(ii) Different observers even when observing the same part of the same object often sense sense-data of that object which seem very unlike each other. Two really unlike sense-data could not be identical with each other, and therefore could not be identical with a third thing—the observed surface. Therefore, either the sense-data of the two observers are not really unlike, although they appear to be so, or at least one of the sense-data is not identical with the observed surface of the object. Thus, when I here and you there see the same part of the same penny, my corresponding sense-datum will seem to me round and your corresponding sense-datum will seem to you elliptical. If the one is really round and the other really elliptical, so that they are really unlike, then they cannot be identical with each other, and therefore they cannot both be identical with a third thing, the observed surface of the penny. Therefore, either one of those corresponding sense-data only *seems* elliptical or one of them is not identical with the observed surface of the penny.

We must next consider two objections which are often made to these two arguments when they are first heard. The first objection is due to confusion. The second needs to be met.

(i) It may be said, "These distortions which trouble you can easily be accounted for. They are due to the action of the laws of perspective and if only you were a little less ignorant of science you would have known this".

But my ignorance is irrelevant here. In the first place, the laws of perspective explain nothing. They are merely statements about the circumstances which will bring about 'distorted' perceptions. For example, one law of perspective may be stated roughly as follows, "The more sideways you look at a penny, the more elliptical will it look". This law tells us how to obtain 'distorted' perceptions; but it does nothing to remove the contradiction between the three propositions:

(1) This (sense-datum) is identical with this surface.
(2) This (sense-datum) is really elliptical.
(3) This surface is round.

(ii) It may be said, "When two observers look at the same penny, they do not strictly see the same part of its surface. One of them sees the 'tails' side and part of the northern edge; the other sees the 'tails' side and part of the southern edge. This appears quite clearly if you take two observers looking at the same cube. It is true that they will both see the top, but the one will see a side which the other does not".

But suppose the penny sunk in sand so that only the 'tails' side is visible and no edges. The resulting corresponding sense-data are still, at least apparently, unlike. Yet in this case the two observers are strictly seeing only the same part of the surface of the penny.

We may then accept as proved the proposition that usually when I see a penny either (α) the corresponding sense-datum is not identical with the observed surface of the penny or (β) the corresponding sense-datum does not really have the characters it is sensed as having.

Can we go a step further and say that this is always so? Such a step is apt to arouse protest when it is first suggested, and yet it is a step which philosophers have seldom hesitated to take. They have thought that if, when I see a table cloth in a rather dim light the corresponding sense-datum is not identical with the observed surface of the table cloth, then it is also not identical with that surface when I see the table cloth in a stronger light. And they have thought that if, when I see a table cloth in a rather dim light the corresponding sense-datum lacks the qualities it is sensed as having, then it does so also when I see that table cloth in a slightly different light. Let us consider these two points.

5.4. ALWAYS EITHER (α) THE CORRESPONDING SENSE-DATUM IS NOT THE SURFACE OR (β) ITS QUALITIES ARE SUBJECTIVE? Which are those most favoured cases of perception in which it may perhaps be supposed that the corresponding sense-datum is both identical with the observed surface and really has the characters it is sensed as having? Although the corresponding sense-data which you obtain[1] by looking at a penny from many points of view are unlike each other in shape, it is easy to see that there is a generic likeness between them all in that they are all sensed as projections of a circle. Up to a certain point, the nearer you approach a penny the more nearly circular does the resulting corresponding sense-datum seem, until the corresponding sense-datum obtained at that certain point seems circular. Nearer than that point the corresponding sense-datum again becomes distorted. May we not say that the corresponding sense-datum which is obtained by an observer at that ideal point is both identical with the surface and really has the characters it is sensed as having, although one or other of these claims fails for a corresponding sense-datum obtained from any other point? Even if we can say this it is not adequate. For

[1] Obtain = sense as having certain sense-characters.

suppose that on Tuesday I view a penny from an ideal point, P; the corresponding sense-datum I then obtain seems round and brown. During the night I develop jaundice. On Wednesday I view that same penny from the same ideal point, P. The corresponding sense-datum which I obtain will indeed seem round, but also it will seem not brown but yellow. The penny, however, has not changed in colour (condition III, p. 139). Therefore either on Tuesday or on Wednesday my corresponding sense-datum was either not identical with the observed surface or lacked the colour it seemed to have.

"But", it will be said, "we all know quite well which day was right. It was Tuesday of course. The corresponding sense-datum that you obtained on Tuesday from P with a healthy eye *was* identical with the observed surface and *really had* the sense-qualities it seemed to have."

This, however, is not enough. For suppose that on Tuesday I saw the penny by candle-light. The colour which a corresponding sense-datum so obtained would seem to have would be different from that which it would seem to have in daylight. And even to mention daylight is not enough. For the day may have been cloudy.[1]

Can we maintain that when a man sees a penny from

---

[1] "I would fain know further from you what certain distance and position of the object, what peculiar texture and formation of the eye, what degree of light is necessary for ascertaining that true colour, and distinguishing it from apparent ones." Berkeley, *The First Dialogue*.

the most favourable position with a well-formed, healthy eye, in a good light, but unaided by microscopes and unhindered by fog, then the corresponding sense-datum which he obtains is both identical with the observed surface and has the characters it seems to have? It must be admitted that these *ideal* perceptions rarely or never occur. But I do not think it can be proved that if one did occur, its corresponding sense-datum would either (α) not be identical with the observed surface, or (β) not independently have the qualities it would be sensed as having.

It may be said: "It is not *impossible* that an ideal perception should occur and its corresponding sense-datum both be identical with the observed surface and independently have the qualities it is sensed as having. But this is an *unplausible* and 'inconsistent' view".

I should agree that it is unplausible to say that, although when I see a thing in bad light my corresponding sense-datum is not identical with the observed surface of the thing, nevertheless, when the light changes, the corresponding sense-datum which I then obtain is identical with the observed surface. I cannot say why I find this unplausible, but I do. I find such a discontinuity, such a popping in and out of the material world on so slight provocation, most objectionable.

On the other hand, I do not find it 'unplausible' or 'inconsistent' or 'discontinuous' to hold that there may be much or little difference between the qualities which a corresponding sense-datum really has and those it is sensed as having, and that this difference may be reduced by big or little amounts according as one approaches by big or little amounts the position, the eye-condition, and lighting of the ideal perception.[1]

To maintain that this *may* be what happens is very different from maintaining that this *is* what happens. In other words: To maintain that we do not know that this is not what happens is very different from maintaining that we do know that this is what happens. It would be a very good thing if we could say that, under certain circumstances, the qualities which sense-data appear to have approach more and more nearly to the qualities they really have; and that, further, we know when this improvement is taking place. For, if this were so, it might be possible to explain how we know so much about material things. And this fortunate feature of this view happens to be an argument in its favour. For our knowledge of material things must be explained somehow, and it is difficult to see how it is to be done unless this view is true.

I have said, however, that we cannot assert that in ideal perceptions the corresponding sense-datum is identical with the observed surface, if we are obliged to admit that sometimes in normal perception the corresponding sense-datum is not identical with the observed surface. Now it has been claimed that it can be proved that the corresponding sense-datum is sometimes not identical with the observed surface. Let us consider this proof.

It has been asserted, and I think we must agree, that if *any* sense-datum is not identical with the surface of an object then this throws doubt on the view that *some*

[1] Compare p. 161.

sense-data are identical with the surfaces of objects. For then we are forced to admit that there are things which have material qualities and yet are not parts of the material world even in the sense in which the surfaces of material things are parts of the material world. And, once this is admitted, we can no longer argue that the corresponding sense-datum of a normal perception must be identical with the observed surface in that perception, on the ground that otherwise it would be such an odd sort of thing—material but not a part of the material world. "Now", it has been said, "it is very doubtful whether the sense-data of a dream are identical with the surfaces of any material objects whatever. When I see a tiger in a dream my striped sense-datum is not part of the surface of a tiger. And is it a part of any other material object?"

Professor Dawes Hicks does, so I gather, believe that even one's dream sense-data are parts of the surfaces of material things.[1] He suggests that one's dream sense-data are parts of one's eye or brain. This suggestion may at first sound incredible, but, when it is carefully stated, it seems much more plausible. It is no doubt incredible that in a dream a man is seeing his brain, in the sense that he is seeing something which is his brain *and* seeing it as his brain.[1] It is even more incredible that a man dreaming of tigers is seeing his brain in this sense and seeing it as having a striped and tigerish part. But it is not nearly so incredible that a man dreaming of a tiger should be visually sensing something which, though he does not know it, is in

[1] *British Contemporary Philosophy*, II, 125.

fact part of his brain. Yet this is all that Professor Dawes
Hicks wants. Even this may seem incredible to some
people, and I admit that I myself feel nervous about it.
But then think what a blessing it would be to have no
sense-data which are not surfaces of material things.[1]

Further, although if sense-data in dreams are not
parts of material things then this weakens the case for
supposing that in normal vision they are, it must
nevertheless be remembered that it *may* be that the
sense-data of dreams and imagination are not parts of
material things while the sense-data in vision of real
things are. Perhaps the tigerish sense-data which I
obtain when I *see* a tiger are parts of a material thing,
although the tigerish sense-data which I obtain when
I *dream* are not.

It has been claimed, however, that sometimes when
I see a real present thing the sense-data that I sense are
not parts of any material thing whatever. If this can
be proved I think we shall have to admit that sense-
data are never identical with the observed surfaces of
material things. It is therefore important to examine
the alleged proof of this statement.

In considering this point we shall have to refer to
abnormal perceptions in which there is often no sense-
datum which we tend to identify with the surface of the
object seen. In these cases, however, there are, as in the
normal cases, always sense-data connected in a peculiarly
intimate way with the object seen. These sense-data are
said to be *of* the object. A sense-datum is *of* an object
when in sensing that sense-datum you are perceiving,

[1] Cf. ambiguity of 'see', p. 135.

however abnormally, that object. Thus the very elliptical sense-data which you get by looking at a penny very much from the side are *of* it; and the sense-data which you get by looking at a penny through coloured spectacles are *of* the penny; and when you see a penny double the two images are both *of* the penny. We can now understand the alleged proof that in some cases, even when sense-data are sense-data of a present object, they are nevertheless not parts of its surface and are not parts of the surface of any other object. This proof runs as follows:

Sometimes I see a penny double (have what is called a 'double image' of it).[1] With a little care I can obtain a double image in which the two images are exactly alike, with nothing to choose between them. They are 'twin' sense-data. When I see a penny double there is no corresponding sense-datum; for there is no sense-datum which is *the* one which I tend to identify with the observed surface. But there are two sense-data, namely the twin images, each of which is *of* the observed surface. We cannot say that there is one sense-datum *sensed as two*; for 'sensed as two' is nonsense. Therefore there *are* two sense-data which are both of the observed surface. And, since there are *two*, they cannot both be identical with the observed surface. Now surely if any sense-datum is ever identical with the surface *of* which it is a sense-datum, then all are, and therefore each of these twin sense-data in double vision is. But they cannot both be. Therefore no sense-datum is ever identical with the surface of which it is a sense-datum. *A fortiori* the corresponding sense-datum is not identical with the observed surface.

[1] It is easier to obtain a double image of a pen or pencil. Focus the eyes on a point behind the pencil.

Moore attaches great weight to the double-image argument, so we must consider it carefully.[1] It proves that sometimes sense-data which are of an object are not identical with the observed surface of *that* object. For the twin sense-data in double visions are of an object, and they are not identical with its observed surface. But does the double-image argument prove that sense-data are sometimes not identical with the surface of *any* object? Professor Dawes Hicks suggests that the twin sense-data of a penny, when I see a penny double, may be identical with the surface, not of the penny, but of the objects which form the background. Suppose that I am looking at a penny lying on a table, and that I begin to see it double. Professor Dawes Hicks suggests that it is parts of the table which I then sense as brown and 'pennyish'. Here once more it is important to realise that it is not suggested that parts of the table appear brown and pennyish to you in the sense that you believe or are tempted to believe that parts of the table are brown and pennyish. The suggestion is only that what appear brown and pennyish to you are in fact parts of the table. This seems to me a quite possible suggestion.

It may be objected that the images are nearer than the background, and that they may be made to approach or recede without the background moving. But our 'perception of distance' is notoriously not an *observation* of something's having the property of distance, but is an *estimation* of something's distance from the appearance of it and neighbouring objects.

[1] Moore, *British Contemporary Philosophy*, II, 220.

We are said to *judge* the distance of a church spire or a man on the horizon. So it is quite possible that, when the images approach, parts of the background are gaining an appearance which leads us to judge them near; while, when they recede, they are losing this appearance and gaining another which leads us to judge them remote. And the objection that in double vision the twins flutter around in a way in which no part of the background is doing may be dealt with on the same lines. There is indeed a sense in which the twins flutter around; but then it may be that, in the unfortunate conditions associated with double vision, first one part of the background is sensed as having a certain set of sense-qualities, and then another part of the background is sensed as having these same sense-qualities. Thus suppose that you see your thumb double and that the twin 'images', though at first steady, begin to move about. Can we not say that these thumbish sense-qualities appeared first in one part of the surface of the background and then in another?

I conclude that the proposition, *In normal perception the corresponding sense-datum is not identical with the observed surface*, is unproved. In other words, I conclude that the view, that in normal perception it is the surface of the observed object which is sensed as having those qualities which something is sensed as having, remains possible. In other words, we began our investigation of normal perceptions with the equation, *Let $x =$ that which is sensed (in the most fundamental sense) as having such and such sense-qualities*. And in spite of the double-image argument and even the argument from the sense-data of dreams, the solution $x =$ *the observed surface*, remains a possible solution. In other words, we are not compelled to take one of one of the *representative* theories of perception.

Therefore it remains possible that normal perceptions approach more and more nearly to revelations, in that while their corresponding sense-data are parts of the observed surfaces, the apparent qualities of these sense-data approach more and more nearly to their real qualities. This possibility will be important in our discussion of the next question.[1]

FURTHER READING

Broad, *The Mind and Its Place in Nature*, Chap. IV.

Moore, *British Contemporary Philosophy*, Vol. II.

Dawes Hicks, Price, Moore, Stebbing. Symposium: *The Nature of Sensible Appearance*. Aristotelian Society Supplementary Vol. VI.

[1] Compare p. 165.

CHAPTER X

KNOWLEDGE OF MATERIAL THINGS

Besides perceiving material things we know a great deal about them. We know particular facts about them, such as the fact that this penny is brown, and we know general facts about them, such as the fact that pennies melt in a hot fire. The knowledge is derived from the perceptions. Something was said in the last chapter about the analysis of the perceptions. We ought to try next to say something about the analysis of the knowledge derived from them, and of the way in which it is derived.

It may be thought very improper to proceed to this complicated discussion without more adequate consideration of the analysis of perception. But I have not room in this book to give both this more adequate analysis of perception and also the discussion of this further question. Yet it is important that one who is beginning philosophy should know something of this further question. For, although an analysis of the perception of material things bears on the question of the analysis of our knowledge about them and on the theory we offer of how this knowledge is obtained, it is also true that the analysis of the knowledge and the theory of how it is to be obtained bears on the analysis of perception. The analysis of perception must not be such that it is impossible that I should know what I do know about material things, for example, that the earth existed before any man was born. It is important that a student of philosophy should realise the unfortunate fact that so many philosophical questions have to be answered all at once.[1]

1. Meaning of 'the Internal Nature of Material Things'. Theories about the knowledge which we have of material things may be more or less sceptical, in the sense that they suppose us to possess much or little knowledge of their internal nature, as opposed to their effects and appearances. By the *internal* nature of material things I mean those qualities of them and relations among them which are *not* of the form *causes a thing which has C* or *appears as having C to someone*. Thus *causes something brown* would not be part of the internal nature of a penny. But suppose that a penny is brown, not merely in the sense that it usually causes brown sense-data or usually appears as brown to most people, but in the sense that it independently itself has that brown character which the sense-data of it certainly either have or appear to have. Then we should

[1] See Stout, *Mind and Matter*, p. 222. "We have no right to assert the nature of anything to be such or such, without being prepared to explain how we can know it to be such or such. On the other hand we have no right to answer the question— How do we know this or that?—in a way which is incompatible with the nature of what is known. The problem is to find a coherent answer to both these questions at once." Here Stout states how questions about what is the case (ontological questions) and questions about our knowledge of what is the case (epistemological questions) bear each upon the other.

say that *brown* is part of the *internal* or *real* nature of the penny. 'Real' is often used here, but it is misleading. For it is quite true of the non-internal characters of the penny that they characterise the penny; the penny certainly has the character *appears brown*, so that in *a* sense *appears brown* is part of the real nature of the penny— no mistake is involved in attributing it to the penny. *Appears brown* is not part of the real nature of the penny, only in the sense that *appears brown* is not an internal character of the penny; because by 'internal' we mean '*not of the form appears such and such or causes such and such*'.

It might be thought that the internal nature of material things must consist of material characters. But you will remember that this is not at all how we defined them. We defined them as such things as trees and tables. And when we so defined them there was no doubt as to their existence. But, if we were to define material things as things whose internal nature is material, then many people would doubt their existence.[1] If we like, we can now substitute for our definition of material things as "such things as trees and tables", the new definition, "the sort of things which sense-data are of". This new definition brings out the relation of the present subject of discussion to the preceding analysis of perception.

We are, then, concerned with the question, "What do we know of the internal nature of those things, whatever they may be, which sense-data are of?"

[1] This is what Berkeley calls the philosopher's sense of the existence of matter.

2. Several Theories.

2.1. THE PHENOMENALIST. He claims that, when we know such a proposition as *There are icebergs at the north pole*, we are knowing merely that there would be certain groups of large, white sense-data at the north pole if we went there. He claims that there is nothing now at the north pole which would be the cause of the sense-data or would cause the sense-data if we went there, or would itself appear large and white if we went there.[1]

2.2. THE AGNOSTIC. He claims that when we know *There are icebergs at the pole*, we are knowing merely that there is something at the pole which is such that *if* we went there it would cause us to sense large white sense-data, or that there is something at the pole which is of such a nature that if we went there we should sense it as large and white. The agnostic claims that we know nothing about this thing except the sort of sense-data it causes or the sort of characters it will appear to have; we know nothing about its internal characters or 'real' nature to use that obscure expression.

---

[1] This view about the analysis of *There is an iceberg at the north pole* is closely associated with view D (p. 145) about the analysis of perception. For view D, unless we allow unsensed sense-data, leads to the view that an unperceived iceberg is a possibility of sensing sense-data. The word 'phenomenalist' is sometimes applied to people who allow unsensed sense-data and then hold that an unperceived object is a set of unperceived sense-data. There is, of course, no logical impossibility in this view, unless sense-qualities are subjective. But I must here neglect it.

2.3. THE MENTALIST OR ONTOLOGICAL IDEALIST.[1] He would probably offer the same analysis of *There is an iceberg at the pole* as that offered by the agnostic. But he adds, astonishingly enough, that we know that the inner nature of the iceberg is spiritual, that that which 'ice-bergish' sense-data are *of*, either itself thinks and feels or is a set of beings who think and feel. Thus Leibnitz held that a material thing is a party of very confused spirits which appear to any moderately confused spirit, such as one of us, as having material characters.

2.4. THE PURE SPATIALIST. The language of some scientists, not when they are doing science but when they are trying to do philosophy, suggests that they believe that the internal characters of material things consist wholly of spatio-temporal characters—say size, shape and speed.

2.5. THE MODERATE MATERIALIST. He believes that the internal characters of material things include not only spatio-temporal characters but also extensive qualities, such as colour.

3. Defence of Moderate Materialism.

3.1. MEANING OF 'EXTERNAL SOURCE'. The defence of moderate materialism cannot be worked out properly and fully here, and very often what looks plausible when stated roughly and in outline becomes quite out

---

[1] The ontological idealist is one who holds that all things are spiritual though some appear material. The epistemological idealist holds that all facts are subjective (p. 148).

of the question when worked out in detail. However, there is no help for it.

The moderate materialist maintains, in opposition to the phenomenalist, that there are some external sources of our sensations. By an 'external source' he means a source other than ourselves or our states. He believes that, when one says "There is an iceberg at the north pole", one is claiming that there is something of such and such a nature now there; he believes that there is something which exists before we have our sensations, something other than us or our states, which helps to cause our sensations. The theory that our sensations have an external source must not be confused with the causal theory of perception, which is the theory that the corresponding sense-datum is merely caused by, and not a part of, the material object. The external source may help to cause a sensation in that the sense-datum sensed in the sensation is *part* of that external source or a manifestation[1] of the external source, or again *merely* an effect of the external source.

The agnostic agrees that my sensations have an external source but disclaims all knowledge of its internal nature. The moderate materialist ·wants to maintain, in opposition to the agnostic, that we have considerable knowledge of its internal nature; and further that, when one says, "There is an iceberg at the north pole", one does not mean merely that there is something at the north pole such that *if* someone went there it *would* appear to be of such and such a nature.

[1] For the manifestation and causal theories of perception see p. 145.

3.2. NEGATIVE OBJECTION TO PHENOMENALISM AND AGNOSTICISM. The moderate materialist has a negative objection to the analysis which the phenomenalist and the agnostic offer of our propositions about material things. He says: However ignorant we may be about the analysis of such a proposition as *There are icebergs at the north pole*, we do know that it is not of the hypothetical sort which the agnostic and the phenomenalist suggest. When one says "There is an iceberg at the north pole" one is stating an *actual* fact, not "a permanent possibility of sensation".

This objection seems to me to be a very important objection. No doubt the hypothetical analyses would never have been offered if it had not been thought impossible to show how any less hypothetical knowledge could be obtained.

Hence the moderate materialist must support his negative objection to the phenomenalist and agnostic theories by trying to show at least in outline (*a*) how we know that there is an external source and (*b*) how we learn something of its internal nature. And in showing how we learn something of this internal nature, he must show that this nature is such as the moderate materialist and not such as the mentalist or the pure spatialist says it is.

3.3. KNOWLEDGE THAT AN EXTERNAL SOURCE EXISTS. He argues as follows: We do not know of the presence of the external sources of our sensations in quite the way in which we know of the presence of the sense-data themselves. The knowledge that there is something more present is 'based on' our knowledge of the sense-data. It is perhaps a mistake to say that we 'infer' from a sense-datum the existence of something beyond it; for 'inference' suggests a process in time—first the premisses and then the conclusion. Nevertheless we do know certain general principles which, together with the behaviour of our sense-data, justify this belief in something beyond the sense-data of the moment. Thus it often happens that each time I open my eyes[1] I see a book, i.e. obtain certain 'bookish' sense-data. My seeing of these sense-data cannot be due wholly to my opening my eyes, because I often open my eyes without obtaining bookish sense-data. On each occasion, therefore, of my seeing the sense-data, there must have been present some other circumstance which, together with the opening of my eyes, caused me to see them. Since the bookish sense-data were similar on each occasion this other circumstance must have been similar on each occasion. Now it is better to suppose that it continued to exist throughout than to suppose that it began to exist each time I opened my eyes, and began in the nick of time to co-operate with them in causing me to see bookish sense-data.[2]

This is all that can be said here in the way of (*a*) out-

[1] Strictly the antecedent like the consequent should be stated in terms of sense-data—the sort of sense-data I have when I feel myself opening my eyes.

[2] For a fuller exposition of this kind of justification of our belief in something beyond the sense-data, see Broad, *Scientific Thought*, p. 422; *The Mind and Its Place in Nature*, p. 460. This argument is often ignored. But has anyone explained what is wrong with it?

lining the way in which our belief that our sensations have external sources is justified. It remains to show (*b*) how we obtain the rather detailed knowledge of the internal nature of those external sources which the moderate materialist claims that we have. For the purpose of justifying this claim to detailed knowledge it is assumed that the external sources either (1) cause sense-data which really have the sense-qualities that we sense, or (2) themselves are sensed as having those sense-qualities, though they usually lack the particular ones which they are sensed as having.

3.4. KNOWLEDGE OF THE INTERNAL NATURE OF THE EXTERNAL SOURCE. The agnostic agrees with the conclusion that our sensations have external sources, but he claims that we are utterly ignorant of the internal nature of these sources. It is worth pointing out, to begin with, that these sources must have some internal nature. For it must be in virtue of some internal character that a thing is *sensed by so and so as having such and such a quality*, or *causes something with such and such a quality*.

Further, there must be an identity of structure or formal similarity[1] between the appearances and what causes them. In other words: If *A*, *B*, *C* and *D* appear to have such and such qualities and relations, then the qualities and relations which cause these appearances must have a formal similarity with the apparent qualities and relations. This means, very roughly, that, although the relations and qualities of the internal

[1] Bertrand Russell, *Analysis of Matter*, Chap. XXIV.

system may be very unlike those of the apparent system, they must be distributed amongst A, B, C and D in a similar way and must arrange A, B, C and D in a similar order. Thus, suppose that the differences in height among a set of children are due to differences of age, so that differences in age appear as differences in height. Suppose that, writing the children in order of height, we have A, D, B, C. Then the children's ages must also run A, D, B, C. Systems which are very unlike may nevertheless be formally similar. Thus a map is not very like the country it maps, and a graph representing the degrees of benevolence possessed by 500 school children is still less like the system of facts which it represents. Yet the map is formally similar to the country, and the graph to the benevolence arrangement. So much for the meaning of 'formally similar'. It is now clear that, if one system is to explain another, then, whether they are like or unlike in point of the elements they contain, there must be formal similarity between the arrangement of the elements of the one and the arrangement of the elements of the other. Thus, suppose that a mirror reflects a certain scene. The nature of the scene explains the nature of the mirror-image, and we may say this even if the mirror distorts. But, however much the mirror distorts, if the nature of the image in it is determined by the nature of the scene before it, there must be formal similarity between the scene and the image. For every difference of quality or relation in the mirror there will be a difference in the corresponding (though not necessarily identical) quality or relation in the scene.

173

This follows from the principle of continuity when that principle is properly stated as follows: If the occurrence of one set of values of a set of variables is the complete cause of the occurrence of a set of values of another or the same set of variables, then each other set of values of the first set of variables will cause a different set of values of the second set of variables—the correspondence between the sets of values of the sets of variables is one-to-one.

The external sources of our sensations appear to have size and shape and to have relations of distance and betweenness. We have just seen that their inner qualities and relations must be formally similar to their apparent qualities and relations. But this tells us very little. I cannot see that it excludes mentalism. For suppose that affection appeared as distance, that a certain sort of feeling appeared as colour, and that numerousness of spirits appeared as size. Then this would provide, I think, for formal similarity. Nevertheless, we are reluctant to believe that affection could appear as distance, and that a change of feeling among a group of spirits could cause a change of colour. Is our reluctance to accept such a doctrine irrational?

If the principle of generic resemblance between cause and effect is true our reluctance to accept a spiritual explanation of material appearances is not irrational but due to our recognition of this causal principle. Given that some external source exists, then from the principle of generic resemblance there follows, not merely the falsity of mentalism, but the truth of moderate materialism. For it follows from the principle of generic resemblance between cause and effect that a system of spatial and extensive characters could be caused only by a system of spatial and extensive characters.[1] And it would seem too, that a thing could appear to have a specific form of a generic character only if and because it had some specific form (the same or different) of the same generic character. From these general principles it follows that, although a thing could cause something round or could itself appear to be round without being round, it could not do so without having some shape, and therefore some size. Hence, since our sense-data in fact are, or appear to be, spatial, their external sources must be really spatial, i.e. spatial in internal nature.[2]

This of course excludes mentalism. But have we excluded the purely spatial theory? This, you will remember, is the theory that the external sources of our sensations have *only* spatial characters. They are large and small, round and rectangular, quick and slow; but they are not red or green, hard or soft, warm or cool, high-pitched or low-pitched, sweet or sour or scented. It has been the custom—following Berkeley—to call the spatio-temporal characters *primary* and the extensive

[1] Professor Broad points out that it looks as if this principle will prove too much. For if *coloured* is a supreme generic character then by the resemblance principle part of the cause of a coloured patch must be coloured. Perhaps the answer is that *coloured* is not a supreme generic character but is a specific form of *extensive sensible quality*. Cf. p. 89, note 1.

[2] Berkeley, *Principles*, CXXXVII.

and other sense-qualities *secondary*.[1] It will be convenient to adopt this terminology here.

The usual reason for saying that we know that the external sources of sensations have primary characters, but do not know that they have secondary characters, is a very poor one. It is pointed out that a thing may first seem of one colour and then, when I get jaundice, of another colour, although it has not really changed in the interval. And it is claimed that the other secondary qualities which things appear to have also vary without alteration in their internal nature.

This argument is a poor one for two reasons. In the first place, the most it could prove is that we do not know *what* secondary qualities things have, not that we do not know that they have *some*. In the second place, the primary qualities which things appear to have, vary without variation in the internal nature of the things; we have seen this when considering the elliptical appearances of the round penny. Yet this, as the pure spatialist himself claims, does not suffice to show that we are ignorant as to what primary qualities are included in the internal natures of things. The pure spatialist, therefore, has failed to prove his statement. But can we disprove it?

This may be done in either of two ways. In the first place, we may argue, as we have done already, that, since the external sources of our sensations either cause sense-data which have extensive qualities, or themselves

[1] Locke also spoke of primary and secondary qualities, but his meaning was different. His secondary qualities were *powers* or *properties*.

appear to have extensive qualities, they must themselves have extensive qualities.

In the second place, a thing cannot have size and shape unless it has some extensive and secondary quality, such as colour, or hardness, or warmth, etc. For to speak of a thing's shape is to say what sort of boundaries its extensive quality has. You can speak of the kind of boundaries which the extensive quality of a thing has without saying *what* that extensive quality is; we do this when we speak of a thing's shape without mentioning its colour or temperature. But a thing cannot have boundaries unless it has *some* extensive quality to be bounded. This leads to the view that the internal nature of material things contains *both* kinds of material characters, namely spatio-temporal characters and extensive qualities. The pure spatialist's theory is therefore false.

Nevertheless there is a truth at the back of it. We are able to *specify* accurately the primary qualities of the external sources. But we have much less knowledge of their secondary qualities. This is due largely to three differences between primary and secondary qualities. (*a*) Primary qualities can be sensed by more than one sense. You can see and also feel the roundness of a penny. (*b*) Primary qualities are effective. "One ball does not *ceteris paribus* behave differently from another when we push it, because it is red and the other blue; but a square body behaves differently from another just because the one is square and the other is round...".[1]

---

[1] Stout, *Mind and Matter*, p. 274.

(c) Primary qualities are quantitative and susceptible of comparison by measurement by superposition. If we are uncertain whether one stick is longer than another, we have only to place them side by side. But we cannot decide by such means whether one thing is warmer than another.

It remains to show how these differences make a difference to the accuracy with which we are able to specify the secondary qualities. This is best brought out by considering how we arrive at our knowledge of the specific shape and size of certain of the external sources of our sensations.

In the first place, there is what Stout calls "the method of standard perceptual appearances". We find that a penny appears sometimes more and sometimes less elliptical; only in the ideal perception does it appear round. In general we take the shape which a thing appears to have in an ideal perception of that thing, and assert that that is its internal shape. This method is also open to us in the case of the secondary qualities. But by itself it is pretty feeble evidence as to the specific internal nature of the external source. In the case of the primary qualities, the method can be supplemented, but in the case of the secondary qualities it cannot. Let us consider these supplementary methods.

(a) I can support my statement that a penny's internal shape is round by noticing that all its other apparent shapes differ from the shape it appears to have when I touch it. For when I touch it it appears round. (b) Further, the hypothesis that the internal shapes of things are identical with the shapes they appear to have in ideal perceptions is extremely successful in enabling us to predict future appearances.[1]

How are we to explain the fact that a flame consumes wood? To explain is to exhibit what takes place as a special case of wider laws, and ultimately of laws which hold for the physical world in general. If we consider the secondary qualities, e.g. the sensible heat of the flame, no advance is possible. The forms and occult qualities of the schoolmen, as Descartes urges, do not help us at all. But, if we regard the process as one in which motion in the particles of the flame determines motion in the particles of the wood, separating them from each other, this explanation is, in principle, possible. For there are laws of the highest generality regulating the motion of bodies, and all transitions from one special configuration to another can be accounted for, in principle, by a special application of these laws to special conditions. Only the primary qualities are found to have objective values[2] which count as causal factors in the executive order of the physical world in general. But how are we to define what these values are? The method of selecting standard perceptual appearances is, by itself, quite insufficient; for in it we are still confined within the limits of sense-perception. But our scientific and even our pre-scientific knowledge of the general causal order indefinitely transcends such limits both in range and precision.[3]

[1] Compare pp. 156, 157.
[2] Stout says in a note, "By *values* I mean values of a variable —the variable size, shape, motion or other general characters of material objects" (*Mind and Matter*, p. 274). By an *objective* value of, for example, shape, Stout means, I think, a value which forms part of the internal nature of the external source as opposed to those values which it appears to have.
[3] *Mind and Matter*, p. 275.

Here, then, are two methods for ascertaining the internal, as opposed to the apparent, characters of the external sources of our sensations. We may select within a certain margin of accuracy (specificness) one apparent value from the many, and say that that is the 'real' or internal nature of the external source. In the case of the primary qualities this claim can be tested by its coherence with the values which appear in touch. And the claim may be further tested by considering its success in enabling us to predict, within a certain margin of accuracy, what values will appear in the future.

You will have noticed the expression "within a certain margin of accuracy". Obviously the narrower this margin the more accurately (specifically) may we know the internal qualities of the external sources of our sensations. Now this margin of accuracy is narrow in the case of the primary qualities; we are able to fix standard appearances of primary qualities and predict and verify future appearances of them with very great accuracy. This is because we are able to measure them one against the other. With the secondary qualities it is otherwise.

Although we are ignorant of *what* secondary qualities a thing has, we know a good deal about these secondary, extensive qualities. In the first place we know that the secondary internal nature of things must be formally similar to their apparent secondary nature. Thus, if we know that *A* appears yellow, *B* orange and *C* red, we do not know that *A* is really yellow, *B* really orange, and *C* really red; but we do know that, whatever the real extensive character corresponding to *coloured* is, *B* has a value of it which falls between those values of it which *A* and *C* possess. In the second place we know what physical phenomena, i.e. primary qualities, are associated with this or that secondary quality. We know that waves of high frequency in the atmosphere are associated with the appearance of the secondary quality *high-pitched*, and we have guessed that different colours are associated with different wave lengths in the luminiferous aether.

4. **Conclusion.** Thus appears in outline how we can know that there is something which is the source of our sensations and how we can know a good deal about its internal nature. There is therefore no need to analyse our statements about material things into hypothetical statements about what would happen if an observer were in a suitable condition. It must be admitted, however, that our statements about the secondary characters of material things are partly hypothetical, though they are partly actual. For example, to say of a cloak, that it is blue, is to say that it actually possesses that extensive character in virtue of which things do in a normal light to a normal observer appear blue.

Such an analysis for secondary qualities is necessary because we cannot learn *what* secondary qualities material things have, although we know that they must have some and we know the formal relations amongst them.

The external source of our sensations of a penny is a penny. Therefore a penny is something which not merely would appear round if viewed by a suitable observer from a suitable point, but is *really* round, i.e. includes roundness in its internal nature, and has certain secondary extensive characters corresponding to brown and cool. Such is the internal nature of that which the corresponding sense-datum corresponds to.

It may be objected that nothing has been done to show that the corresponding sense-datum of a penny is not itself the external source of one's sensations of a penny. Perhaps in a sense it is. For perhaps the corresponding sense-datum is identical with the surface of the penny. But in a sense it is not. For when I see first one side of a penny and then the other, I am sure that the corresponding sense-datum in my first sensation is not the same as that in my second sensation when I see the other side of the penny; and yet I am sure that the same penny is the source of both sensations.

This statement cannot be justified here. Nor can it here be shown how we reach the knowledge that the penny is a three-dimensional object. I can only suggest that the sensations of touch as we explore an object by moving our hands over it, up and down, left and right, inwards and outwards, together with seeing several sides of an object at once, are important factors. And I cannot help suggesting that we know from the first that the corresponding sense-datum has another side.

5. **Summary of the last two chapters.** We started by trying to find the analysis of such a fact as is commonly expressed by "I see a penny". This fact we found contains (i) an observer, (ii) an object,

(iii) the observed surface of the object, (iv) certain sense-qualities, and (v) the corresponding sense-datum which is what is sensed as having the sense-qualities.

We found that either (α) the corresponding sense-datum is usually not identical with the observed surface of the object, or (β) the corresponding sense-datum usually lacks the qualities it is sensed as having. For (1) the qualities which it is sensed as having are usually incompatible with the qualities of the surface, and (2) the qualities which different observers sense their corresponding sense-data as having are usually incompatible with one another.

We could not accept (α) without allowing that the corresponding sense-datum is never part of the surface of an object. We could, however, accept (β) and claim that under favourable conditions the apparent qualities of the corresponding sense-datum approach more and more to its real qualities.

The double-image argument failed to prove that it is (α) which we must accept. Hence we may claim that in 'ideal' perceptions the corresponding sense-datum may both be identical with the observed surface and really have the qualities it appears to us to have.

Leaving the analysis of perception unfinished, we passed to the question of the analysis of our knowledge about material things, and whether we know anything of their internal or real qualities as opposed to the qualities they either cause sense-data to have or themselves appear to have.

The extreme phenomenalist claims that nothing exists but the sense-data of the moment and thus holds that there is nothing behind them to have an internal nature. The agnostic admits that there is something which is the external source of our sense-data, but disclaims all knowledge of its internal nature. We decided that there does exist an external source of our sense-data—and we *assumed* that either they are merely effects of that source or part of its surface. We decided, too, that we are not entirely ignorant of its internal nature, and we tried to show in outline what knowledge we have of this and how it is gained. In doing so we refuted the doctrines of the mentalist, who claims that everything is spiritual in its internal nature, and the pure spatialist, who maintains that material things are the forms of nothing.

FURTHER READING

Berkeley, *Dialogues*.
Stout, *Mind and Matter*, Book III.

CHAPTER XI

JUDGMENT AND TRUTH

1. **The Problem.** Minds own material things and perceive material things, and also they make true and false statements about material and other things. We shall consider the problem of truth quite generally and without special reference to judgments about material things as opposed to semi-material things like animals and human beings.

Some philosophers have spoken as if the problem of truth is the problem of how we come to know the truth. This is not at all the problem which we shall discuss. I do not wish to say that such a problem is not properly called the problem of truth; but I should prefer to call it the problem of knowledge, and to reserve the title 'problem of truth' for the easier problem which we shall now discuss.

By 'the problem of truth' I mean the problem of setting out fully and clearly what is being said of a statement when we call it true; we want a definition of "It is true that Cameronian beat Orpen".

This is clearly a very different problem from that of how we come to know that Cameronian beat Orpen. But, though very different, the two questions bear on one another. We must not analyse *true* in such a way that we can never know anything to be true; for we certainly do sometimes know a statement to be true.

As in the case of the analysis of perception, the analysis must be made to fit the facts, not the facts the analysis.

Some people have claimed that it is very difficult to find a definition of 'true' which will permit of our knowing to be true what we do know to be true and which will permit of our knowing to be false what we know to be false. I am unfortunately incapable of seeing that this is difficult: but you will judge for yourself when the suggested definitions of 'true' have been set out.

1.1. TRUE IS A RELATIONAL CHARACTER. 'True' might at first be thought to be a name for a simple character like 'red'. But it is not. It is a short word which stands for a complicated relationship to other things. And we want to know (*a*) what relation a statement must have to other things and (*b*) what those other things must be, if that statement is to be true.

2. **Conditions of Correct Analysis of Truth.** It will be obvious that, if what is meant by 'true' is a certain relationship, then (i) whenever a statement is true it must stand in that relationship, and (ii) whenever a statement stands in that relationship it must be true. In other words: If the word 'true' means what some other word or phrase, '*P*', means, then (i) whenever we can apply 'true' to a statement we can apply '*P*' to it, and (ii) whenever we can apply '*P*' to a statement, we can apply 'true' to it. Thus if 'true' = 'fits the facts' and the statement "Cats play chess" fits the facts, then that statement is true.

On the other hand, two words may each apply to the

same things and yet not mean the same. Thus every featherless biped is a human being and conversely. But when we say "Tony is a human being" we do not *mean* that he is a featherless biped. Again, since God makes no mistakes every statement which God believes is true; and since He knows all things every true statement is believed by God. Yet 'true' does not mean 'believed by God'.[1] For it is not self-contradictory (though it may well be a mistake) to say, "This belief is true but God does not believe it".

If, then, a phrase, '*P*', is to mean the same as the word 'true', then it is necessary that (i) every statement which has *P* should be true, and (ii) that every statement which is true should have *P*, and (iii) that it should be self-contradictory to say of a statement that it is true but lacks *P*.

There are roughly speaking three kinds of theories about the definition of 'true':

I. Pragmatic Theories, e.g. True = serves our purposes.

II. Coherence Theories, e.g. True = coheres with other beliefs.

III. Accordance Theories, e.g. True = accords with facts.

3. **Pragmatism.** 'Pragmatism' is used in philosophy for many different theories, and not all of these are about the analysis of *true*. Perhaps indeed none of

[1] This view leads to the consequence: *The proposition "God does not exist is true* entails both *God does not exist* and *God does exist"*. In connexion with self-contradiction, see pp. 57–8.

these theories are about the analysis of *true*; perhaps they are all concerned with the circumstances which tend to make us believe that a statement is true. I say this partly because many of the statements made by pragmatists seem very foolish when they are interpreted as statements about the definition of 'true' and not at all foolish when interpreted as statements about the circumstances which tend to make us believe that a statement is true or tend to justify our belief that a statement is true. On the other hand, as you will see, one of the leaders of pragmatism has used language which suggests that he is concerned with the definition of 'true'.

3.1. 'TRUE' MEANS 'VERIFIABLE'. William James says, "true ideas are those which we can assimilate, corroborate, verify. False ideas are those that we cannot".[1] But suppose a friend accuses me of not arriving on the day I had promised. I reply that I made no such promise. Our statements are contradictory—he says I promised to arrive on Friday, I deny it—therefore one of our statements must be true. But neither is verifiable.[2] Even if I promised by letter, the letter may have been destroyed.

It may be objected that one of us is remembering correctly and that his memory is verifying his statement. But this theory breaks down when we apply it to

[1] *Pragmatism*, p. 201. Quoted by Moore, *Philosophical Studies*, "Essay on William James' Pragmatism".

[2] 'Verifiable' is not used in the sense in which the logical positivists now use it.

universal statements such as, *Druids conducted human sacrifices* and *It is not the case that Druids conducted human sacrifices*. One of these statements must be true, but neither is verifiable by memory or any other means.

It may be objected that neither statement can justifiably be made, and that what James meant was that no statement *can be known to be true* unless it is verifiable. We have already decided that we are concerned not with what justifies a statement, but with the meaning of 'true'. And we have found two statements, one of which must be true and neither of which is verifiable. Therefore 'true' does not mean 'verifiable' (by condition (ii), p. 187).

3.2. 'TRUE' MEANS 'USEFUL'. James also says, "The true is the expedient". If we hold a false belief it usually ends in some inconvenience—we miss our train or meet the police. But much more than this is required if 'true' is to mean 'useful'. For, by condition (ii), p. 187, if 'true' means 'useful' then no false statement can be useful.

It is perhaps plausible to maintain that no universal statement which is false can usefully be believed. But even this is far from certain.

And to hold that no *particular* false belief has ever been useful is out of the question. For suppose that a man believes his wife is ill and consequently returns home. She is quite well, so that his belief is not true. But if the inmates of the boarding house at which he was staying all die of ptomaine poisoning from the supper he would have shared had he not left when he did, then surely his false belief is useful?

Again, it is not self-contradictory to assert *The false belief in immortality is useful*. This statement may be mistaken; but it is not self-contradictory. Yet, if 'true' means 'useful', then the statement means *The useless belief in immortality is useful*, and thus is not merely false but self-contradictory. Since it is not self-contradictory, 'true' cannot mean useful (by condition (iii), p. 187).

4. **Coherence.** This theory is sometimes stated loosely in the form: *To say of a belief that it is true is to say that it coheres with other beliefs.* This will never do. The beliefs of a lunatic notoriously cohere with his other beliefs. The megalomaniac believes that he is the King of France. This belief is coherent with, i.e. is not incompatible with, his belief that he is washing the floor of the lunatic asylum. Our other beliefs render unlikely the statement that the King of France is washing the floor of the lunatic asylum, but they are not incompatible with this statement. And even the unlikelihood the megalomaniac reduces by believing that he is the victim of a plot.

However, the statement of the Coherence theory can easily be tightened up so as to avoid this objection. It may be restated as follows: *A belief is true when it coheres with the biggest system of coherent beliefs.*[1]

[1] This is an unfairly simplified account of the coherence theory. But I believe that a more careful account would still be open to this refutation.

But this theory also is false. For suppose (1) that there are only two people in the world, namely A and B; (2) that A's beliefs are coherent with one another and that B's beliefs are coherent with one another; (3) that A believes the contradictory of everything that B believes, while B believes the contradictory of everything that A believes. If 'true' means 'coheres with the biggest coherent set of beliefs', then from (1), (2) and (3) it would follow that neither of two contradictory beliefs is true.

For from (1), (2) and (3) it would follow in the first place that no belief is true; since from (1), (2) and (3) it follows that there is no coherent set of beliefs bigger than any other. This can be proved as follows. From (1), (2) and (3) it follows that there is no coherent set of beliefs bigger than the set of A's beliefs. For [by (1)] there are no beliefs but those of A and B. Now, if we take *all* A's beliefs, we cannot add any of B's; since each of these is incompatible with one or other of A's [by (3)]. Therefore, since coherence implies consistency, none of B's beliefs could be in the same coherent set with A's beliefs. Similarly, if we take *all* B's beliefs, we cannot add any of A's beliefs. Finally, if we take *some* of A's beliefs and add to these some of B's, then we must reject as many of B's beliefs as we have included of A's, since for every one of A's included we must exclude that one of B's which contradicts it; and we must also reject as many of A's beliefs as we add of B's, since for every one of B's we add, we must exclude that one of A's which contradicts it. It follows then from (1), (2) and (3) that there is no coherent set of beliefs bigger than A's. It follows also that A's set of coherent beliefs is not the biggest of all coherent sets; since the set of B's beliefs is coherent [by (2)] and equal [by (3)]. Thus does it follow in the first place from (1), (2) and (3) that there is no biggest coherent set of beliefs and therefore, *if* 'true' means 'coherent with the biggest coherent set of beliefs', no true belief.

From (1), (2) and (3) it follows, in the second place, that there are two contradictory beliefs, namely one of A's and that one of B's which contradicts it. Combining these results we have: If 'true' means 'coheres with the biggest coherent set of beliefs', then from (1), (2) and (3) it would follow that neither of two contradictory beliefs is true.

Since no such absurd consequence does follow from (1), (2) and (3) we must conclude that 'true' does not mean 'coheres with the biggest coherent set of beliefs'.

It has been objected to this argument that there are not in fact only two people in the world whose beliefs oppose one another in the way suggested.

This objection arises from a failure to grasp the logical form of the argument. The argument does *not* contain as a premiss the obviously false statement that there are only two people and that their beliefs form opposing systems. It contains the premiss that such a hypothesis is not impossible.

It may be said, "But it *is* impossible. We *know* that there are not just two people whose beliefs, etc."

This difficulty arises from the ambiguity of 'possible'. When in the argument it is claimed that the hypothesis made up of (1), (2) and (3) is possible, it is not meant that this hypothesis is not certainly false. It is certainly false. What is meant is that (1), (2) and (3) would not lead to contradiction—that they would not entail the logical impossibility that neither of two contradictory beliefs is true.

It must, of course, be understood that by 'contradictory' I mean 'contradictory' and not 'contrary' or 'opposite'. It is perfectly possible that neither of two contrary beliefs should be true. Thus suppose I say "All men are liars", and you say "No men are liars"; then our beliefs are contrary and it is perfectly possible that we should both be wrong in that some men are liars and some are not. But if I say "All men are liars", and you say "It is not the case that all men are liars", then you contradict me; and not only must one of us be wrong, but also one of us must be right.

The argument may be restated briefly as follows: Let us call two sets of beliefs related as were those of *A* and *B*, *opposing systems*. That is, α and β are opposing systems if each is a set of coherent beliefs and each member of the one is contradicted by just one member of the other.

We wish to prove that 'true' cannot mean 'coheres with a set of coherent beliefs bigger than any other'.

I. If (i) 'true' were to mean 'coheres with the biggest coherent set', then (ii) that (*a*) all beliefs should fall into two opposing systems would entail that (*b*) neither of two contradictory beliefs is true. [For if (*a*) then there would be two contradictory beliefs but no biggest coherent set. Since the systems are opposing there would obviously be two contradictory beliefs. And there would be no biggest coherent set: for by (*a*) there are no beliefs not in one or other system; and, since the systems are opposing, it is impossible to obtain by selection from them a coherent set bigger than either; and neither system is bigger than the other.]

II. But that there should be just two people and that one should believe the contradictory of everything that the other believes would not entail the absurd consequence that neither of two contradictory beliefs is true, i.e. (*a*) does not entail (*b*), i.e. (ii) is false.

Therefore 'true' does not mean 'coheres with the biggest coherent set', i.e. (i) is false.

Another, and sufficiently monstrous, though not logically absurd, consequence of the view that 'true' means 'coheres with the biggest coherent set of beliefs' is that if there were two systems of belief of equal size, then neither would be true.[1]

It may be urged that if two scientific hypotheses each account for or cohere with an equal number of facts or other beliefs, then neither is true for us. But either (α) this is false, or (β) it means that we could not know which was true. And if (β) then the argument is guilty of that old confusion between the question of the definition of 'true' and theories about how we come to know whether a belief is true. There remain the Accordance theories of truth.

5. **Accordance.** The accordance theory of truth is true. Indeed it is only *too* obviously true. This is a paradoxical way of saying that the definition offered,

[1] See Russell, *The Problems of Philosophy*, p. 191.

though correct, does nothing to reveal the fundamental structure of what we express about a statement when we say that it is true. Thus we may define 'wealth' as 'riches'; but this definition, though correct, is unenlightening.

We may notice to begin with that "It is true that Cameronian beat Orpen" is often expressed by "It is a fact that Cameronian beat Orpen", or by "The statement that Cameronian beat Orpen is a fact". Let us consider the latter translation. If we say "The statement that Cameronian beat Orpen is a fact", the fact we have in mind is one about Cameronian and Orpen. But obviously we do not mean that the statement is *identical* with this fact. You and I make the statement, but we do not make the fact. When we say that the statement *is* a fact, we mean that it "*is in accordance with a fact*". Hence we may now write: "The view, the statement, the proposition, that Cameronian beat Orpen, is true" means "The proposition that Cameronian beat Orpen is in accordance with the facts".

The analysis of truth is carried thus far by non-philosophers. For it is quite usual in ordinary speech to substitute the expression 'in accordance with the facts' for 'true'. The only people who have objected to this definition are philosophers. They say, "What do you mean by 'facts'? What do you mean by 'accordance'?" And they appear to imagine that if we cannot answer, then this inability of ours is a reason for believing the definition incorrect. It is not. Our inability is at most a reason for saying that the definition will remain unenlightening. Even this charge, however, is false. For the definition is not unenlightening. It is no more unenlightening than the definition 'coheres with beliefs' would be if it were correct. And 'accords with facts' has the advantage of correctness.

However, we are not unable to carry the analysis further. As to facts, a great deal could be said. There is this kind of fact and that; and then, too, there is not this and that kind of fact; and finally, perhaps, there are no facts at all but only events. But it takes a long time to put all this into non-paradoxical language.[1] Besides, the analysis of truth can be carried a long way without doing so. It is necessary only to repeat that in this discussion the word 'fact' is used in a way which no one makes any fuss about when it occurs in the *Strand* or *Windsor* magazine.[2] As to 'proposition' and 'accordance' more can and shall be said. Most people agree that 'true' means 'accords with fact', but there is considerable difference of opinion about the analysis of *proposition* and *accordance*. This disagreement generates the different kinds of accordance theory.

5.1. ANALYSIS OF 'PROPOSITION'. We will simplify the problem at the outset by stating that we are concerned only with the truth of *elementary* or *complete* propositions, not with the truth of *general* or *incomplete* propositions. I have already explained roughly the distinction between elementary or complete sentences and general or incomplete sentences.[3] Elementary sentences are those which like "Cameronian beat

[1] For one attempt at this see "Logical Constructions", *op. cit.* p. 20.

[2] See p. 20.   [3] See p. 21.

Orpen" contain only proper names, verbs, adjectives and prepositions. General sentences are those of the form "Something which has S has P", "The thing which has S has P", or "Everything which has S has P". (It may be noticed that common nouns are often used instead of an expression of the form, "Thing which has S". Thus 'man' = 'thing which has humanity'.) An elementary proposition is the sort of proposition which a man asserts when he utters an elementary sentence. This is enough to enable people to know when we should call a proposition 'elementary'. But it provides no analytic definition of *propositions*, throws no light on their 'ultimate' nature, and does nothing to reveal the fundamental structure of what we express when we speak of propositions. We must now try to do something towards filling these gaps.

5.11. On the one hand, we must avoid that error against which the Oxford logicians fought so long. This is the error of supposing that a proposition has a peculiar specific form of *being*, a form different from that of things on the one hand and of their states on the other, but not, I gather, entirely unlike that of universals. These peculiar things which have been called 'asserta' (as opposed to assertions, which are events), 'meanings', 'possibilities of assertion', float about out of time, waiting to be asserted. I want to persuade you that this view is unnecessary. I am convinced that in some way propositions are reducible to, though not necessarily identical with, things and the events which make up their life-histories.

5.12. On the other hand, we must not allow the pendulum to carry us too far, so that we identify each proposition with that delightfully plain thing the sentence, which is made up of the marks or noises with which the proposition is expressed.[1] A proposition is not the words we utter but what we mean by our words. Frenchmen and Englishmen use *different* sentences to express the *same* proposition.

5.13. And we must not fall into the error against which the Cambridge logicians fought. This is the error of supposing that when I assert the proposition that Cameronian beat Orpen, my proposition is identical with that particular event in my history which is my assertion or judgment now that Cameronian beat Orpen. This event in my history or particular fact about me is again delightfully 'plain'. And it is closely associated with my proposition, indeed my proposition is *reducible* to this judgment and others which are like it in a certain respect. But it is not identical with it. My judgment now that Cameronian beat Orpen in 1931 is a mental event and is equivalent to the particular fact, *I am judging now that Cameronian beat Orpen in* 1931. It is clear that I am a constituent of this fact, that the relation of judging is its component, and that it is a fact about the present time. It follows that it is not identical with the proposition that Cameronian beat Orpen. For (1) suppose that you and I both assert that Cameronian beat Orpen. Then it is correct to say that we both assert the same proposition—your proposition

[1] See Mace, *Principles of Logic*, Chap. II.

is the same as mine. But your judgment is not the same as mine. One judgment is yours and not mine, and the other is mine and not yours; more explicitly, the particular fact that you are now judging that Cameronian beat Orpen contains you as a constituent, while the particular fact that I am now judging that Cameronian beat Orpen contains me as a constituent. (2) Suppose that I first to-day and then to-morrow judge that Cameronian beat Orpen. There would then be two judgments each at a different time. But there would be only one proposition. We conclude then, that when I assert that Cameronian beat Orpen, we cannot identify that proposition with my judgment, meaning by 'my judgment'[1] the particular fact that I am now judging that Cameronian beat Orpen.

5.14. Can we *reduce* that proposition to my judgment? No. But we can reduce the proposition to a certain set of judgments. In other words, the proposition is an abstraction from a set of judgments; it is a set of judgments in abstraction from (*a*) the particular people who make them and (*b*) the particular times at which they are made. By these abstractions the two objections (*a*) and (*b*) mentioned above, against the *identification* of a proposition with a particular judgment, are rendered powerless against the view that a proposition is *reducible to* or an *abstraction from* a set of judgments.

[1] The discussion of this subject is sometimes obscured by using 'judgment' in exactly the way in which 'proposition' is used. Of course I am not a constituent of my proposition unless I judge about myself.

"But", it may be asked, "why say in this utterly obscure way that a proposition is 'reducible to, i.e. an abstraction from', a set of judgments? Can't you say that a proposition *is* a set of judgments?"

The response to this is (1) to prove that a proposition is not identical with a set of judgments, and (2) to admit and remove the obscurity of 'reducible to'.

(1) A set of judgments contains the people who make them. But a proposition does not contain the people who assert it. And a set of judgments has many members, but a proposition has not.

(2) To say "The proposition Cameronian beat Orpen is reducible to a set of judgments in abstraction from those who make them and the times at which they are made", is to say the following: "When I utter a sentence beginning 'The proposition Cameronian beat Orpen...' then I am speaking about a set of judgments which I describe without mentioning the names of those who make them or the times at which they are made." In other words: When I say something about a proposition I am saying something, though not quite the same thing, about a set of judgments. It is important to notice the clause 'not quite the same thing'; for this is where this view is different from the view that a proposition is identical with a set of judgments. For if a proposition were identical with a set of judgments, then whatever we said of the proposition, that *same* thing could be said of the set of judgments; and this is what we have seen can *not* be done.

We conclude: "The proposition Cameronian beat Orpen accords with a fact" means "Any judgment made by *any* body at *any* time to the effect that Cameronian beat Orpen will *accord* with a fact". The sense in which a judgment "accords with a fact" is slightly different and more fundamental than the sense in which a proposition "accords with a fact": so we write it in italics. But we need not bother further about this slight difference here, and we may proceed at once to analyse what is meant by saying of an elementary judgment, such as *I judge now that Cameronian beat Orpen in* 1931, that it *accords* with a fact.

5.2. ANALYSIS OF 'ACCORDANCE'. My judgment that Cameronian beat Orpen is equivalent to the particular fact that I am judging now that Cameronian beat Orpen in 1931.[1] The fact with which this judgment-fact accords is obviously the fact *Cameronian beat Orpen in* 1931. And it is easy to see in outline what 'accords' means here. For example, we know at once that *I judge now that Cameronian beat Orpen* does not accord with *Sandwich beat Orpen*; nor does it accord with *Orpen beat Cameronian*. But can we say in detail what this relation of *accordance* is?

5.21. Is it the relation of *identity*? Obviously not. For (i) the judgment contains me—the judge or subjective constituent—while the fact does not. (ii) The judgment contains the relation *judging* as component, while the fact does not. (iii) The *component* in the fact, namely *beat*, is a *constituent* in the judgment.

5.22. Does my judgment *accord* with the fact in the sense that it *includes* it? No. For if my judgment that

[1] For equivalence of facts and events see p. 31.

Cameronian beat Orpen included the fact that Cameronian beat Orpen, then the judgment would not occur at all without the fact; for it could not occur without what it includes. Hence on this view it would follow logically from the fact that *I judge* that *S* is *P*, that *it is a fact* that *S* is *P*, and therefore that my judgment is true. But it is notorious that we make false judgments.

5.23. It seems to me quite obvious that the correct analysis of *accords* is as follows: "My judgment that Cameronian beat Orpen *accords* with a fact" means "There is some fact such that (i) the elements in that fact are identical with the objective constituents in my judgment, (ii) the order of the elements in the judgment *reflects* the order of the elements in the fact".

As to condition (i). By the objective constituents in a judgment is meant those of its constituents other than the judge;[1] i.e. those of its elements other than the judge and the relation of judging. It is clear that the fact which accords with my judgment that Cameronian beat Orpen must contain as elements Cameronian, Orpen and *beat*—nothing else will do.

As to condition (ii). It is clear that condition (i), though necessary, is insufficient. For, if it were a fact that Orpen beat Cameronian this fact would satisfy condition (i), since its elements would be identical with the objective constituents in my judgment. And

[1] The times of judging and time judged about are neglected. For 'objective constituent' see Moore, *Facts and Propositions*. Aristotelian Society Suppl. Vol. VII, p. 183.

yet it would not accord with my judgment. This is because my judgment would have Cameronian and Orpen "the wrong way round", that is, the order of the elements in my judgment would not *reflect* the order of the elements in the fact.

The order of the elements in a judgment *reflects* the order of the elements in a fact when what occupies place number n in the fact occupies place number $n-2$ in the judgment. It must be understood that the elements in a fact are numbered from left to right. Thus we have the fact $This_1$ is red_2 and the judgment-fact I_1 $judge_2$ $this_3$ is red_4. And we have $This_1$ $adjoins_2$ $that_3$ which accords with I_1 $judge_2$ $this_3$ $adjoins_4$ $that_5$. And we have A_1 $gave_2$ B_3 to C_4 which accords with I_1 $judge_2$ A_3 $gave_4$ B_5 to C_6.

Every judgment is a fact with at least three terms. It should be noticed, however, that a judgment may contain any greater number of terms.

When I *observe* that a has R to b, that four-termed fact contains the independent two-termed fact that a has R to b. We have already decided that when I *judge* that a has R to b that four-termed fact does not contain the fact that a has R to b. And this is very proper. For from *I observe that this adjoins that* it does logically follow that this adjoins that; while from *I judge that this adjoins that* it does not logically follow that this adjoins that.

It may be objected to the theory stated above, which may be called the Correspondence theory, that, though it leaves more room for error than the identity and inclusion theories, it yet fails to leave room enough, because it makes the judgment contain the elements of the fact.

It must be emphasized that considerable room is left for error. In my judgment that a has R to b, I may be mistaken in that it is not a which has R to b but b which has R to a, or in that not a but c has R to b or in that it is not a which has R to b but c which has R to d. It must, however, be admitted that according to the theory which I have called the correspondence theory of truth, there cannot be error in that one of the elements of the fact referred to does not exist. For, since they are constituents of the judgment, they must exist. But this possibility of error does not occur until we reach general or incomplete judgments. And it must be remembered that the part of the correspondence theory stated above applies only to elementary judgments.

My incomplete judgment that *something* beat Orpen accords with the fact *Cameronian beat Orpen* in that (i) this fact contains the objective constituents of my judgment and (ii) the order of the elements in the judgment reflects the order of the elements in the fact (provided that in counting the elements of the judgment, *something* is counted as if it were an element).

My incomplete judgment *Some pink horse beat Orpen* may be false on the ground that though its main assertion *Something beat Orpen* is true, its subsidiary assertion *Something was a pink horse* is false. It would then be said to be false because its "subject does not exist".

That is the bare outline of the theory of the slightly modified definitions of 'true' required for incomplete or general judgments and propositions.

6. **Summary.** (i) We set out to define 'true'; not to learn how we make sure that a proposition is true.

(ii) Utility and Coherence we found useful tests of truth but quite hopeless as definitions.

(iii) We accepted the ordinary view that a proposition is true when it accords with facts.

(iv) A proposition is not an event nor a thing nor a fact nor a subsistent meaning. It is *reducible to* or an *abstraction from* judgments—not at all in the sense that judgments contain it but in the sense that—

(v) To speak of the proposition that *a* has *R* to *b* is a shorthand way of speaking about every judgment with *a*, *b*, and *R* as objective constituents arranged in the order *a*, *R*, *b*, no matter who makes the judgment nor at what time it is made.

(vi) Hence "The proposition that *a* has *R* to *b* is true" means "Every judgment of the form *x judges at time t that a has R to b* accords with a fact.

(vii) The judgment is not identical with the fact nor does it include it.

(viii) The judgment accords with the fact in that (*a*) the objective constituents of the judgment are the elements of the fact, (*b*) what occupies place *n* in the fact occupies place *n*-2 in the judgment.

FURTHER READING

Pragmatism: James, *Pragmatism*.
Coherence: Joachim, *The Nature of Truth*.
Correspondence: Russell, *The Problems of Philosophy*, Chap. XII.

Mental and Material Facts. It is claimed by Professor Stout and Mr Mace, I believe, that every mental fact not only *does* contain a material fact but *must* contain one. *This is larger than that* is a material fact and *I perceive that this is larger than that* is a mental fact which contains it, while *I realise that I perceive that this is larger than that* contains a mental fact which contains a material fact. According to Stout and Mace every mental fact contains directly or indirectly a material fact. They have in mind, I suppose, some such argument as follows: Every mental fact involves consciousness, and you cannot have consciousness without having consciousness of something. Hence every mental fact is of the form *I know that so and so is such and such*, or, more conveniently, *I know that S has P*. Now every fact is either mental or material. If *S is P* is material then *I know that S is P* contains directly a material fact. If it is mental then it is of the form, *S knows that S_1 has P_1*; and the original fact becomes, *I know that S knows that S_1 has P_1*. And now as to *S_1 has P_1*. If it is material then the original fact indirectly contains a material fact. If it is mental it is of the form *S_1 knows that S_2 has P_2*; and the original fact becomes *I know that S knows that S_1 knows that S_2 has P_2*. It is now clear that this series is endless unless at last the fact known is not mental and is therefore material. But if at last the fact known is material, then each earlier term in the series contains directly or indirectly a material fact. Such a series would be vicious if endless. Therefore every mental fact does contain directly or indirectly a material fact.

I should admit that such an endless series would be vicious. And I think it probable that every fact is either mental or material. But (i) this is not necessary. Hence it is not necessary that every mental fact should contain a material fact, even if it must contain a non-mental fact. (ii) It is not at present quite clear to me that there cannot be consciousness without consciousness of something, that is, that every mental fact is or contains a fact of the form *X knows that S has P.*

APPENDIX II

Universals and Particulars. (i) There is another way of distinguishing between universals and particulars. Among particulars exact likeness is not identity. Suppose two pennies whose shape, colour, hardness, etc., are exactly the same, and let them be alone in a sunless and cloudless blue so that they completely agree not only in their qualities but also in their relations to what is around them—they are exactly alike. But they are not identical: there are still two pennies. Let us express the fact that the two pennies have the same qualities and relations by saying that they are *similar* and let us say that the two pennies though similar are diverse. It is clear that among particulars similarity does not vanish into identity, in other words, diversity does not imply dissimilarity.

Among universals it is otherwise. They are like each other and other than one another in a sense in which particulars are not; and in this sense in which they are like and *are* other, exact likeness is identity and diversity is unlikeness. Red and yellow are unlike; a slightly orangish red and a slightly orangish yellow are less unlike; a still more orangish red and a still more orangish yellow are still less unlike. When we reach a point at which there is no unlikeness there are no longer two hues but only one, namely orange. This makes clear what is meant by saying that, in the sense applicable to universals, exact likeness vanishes into identity. Let us call this relation between universals 'qualitative diversity', although the name wrongly suggests that the relation is a species of diversity. In fact the relation is neither a species of diversity nor a species of dissimilarity, but comes between them or combines them. Universals may *also* be similar and dissimilar. Thus cold and black may agree in the respect that they both characterise a certain liquid.

We have now distinguished between diversity (numerical), dissimilarity (unlikeness in this or that respect), and qualitative diversity (i.e. the unlikeness between universals which implies or includes the fact that there are two of them). And then I spoke in the text of an inner difference between universals and particulars. This inner difference is akin to qualitative diversity among universals, but it is not quite the same. For one thing qualitative diversity is susceptible of degrees.[1]

(ii) Perhaps there is still another kind of difference. For how about selves—are they particulars? A suggestion by Mr Mace seems to me plausible, namely that we should recognise universals (green and happy) and places (*here's* and *there's*) and selves (*you's* and *me's*) as ultimately different types or elements in the world. To this I would add the following. The selves are not merely dissimilar to one another, they also have qualitative diversity. I think this because it seems to me that it is logically impossible that there should be two

---

[1] In my opinion, the neglect of inner likeness and the assumption that the difference between universals and particulars must be a dissimilarity, misled Ramsey in his work on universals. See *The Foundations of Mathematics*, pp. 112–37.

selves exactly alike; it seems impossible in rather the way that it is impossible that there should be two hues exactly alike. There might be two selves precisely similar in that every character of the one was a character of the other. Yet there would be a *significant* diversity between them, in a way in which there would be no *significant* diversity between two exactly similar places. And there would be a *significant* diversity between two hues even if every character of the one were also a character of the other. Is this what was meant by the statement that individuals are 'concrete universals'?

INDEX

Abnormal perception, 135, 159
Abstraction, 199
Accordance, 194–205
Adrian, E. D., 50
Agnostic, 167
Analysis, Preface; nature of, 1–3; and science, 17, 18, 37; method for, 138; conditions of, 138, 185
Analytic psychology, 16–18
Analytic vocabulary, 20–33
Animism, Stout's, 100
Appears, applied to sense-data, 149; to material things, 166
Aspect of, 97; 125
Atomic facts, 20 n. 2
Awareness, 11

Background, 161
Beethoven, 16
Behaviourism, 56–8
Belief, 190–205
Berkeley, 148; 166; 175; 184
Blame, and freewill, 114–18; and causation, 118–31
Body and mind, Preface; 37–9, 103–9; nature of events in, 40–52; correlations with mind, 59–64; causal connexions with mind, 65–102
Broad, C. D., Preface; 33; 53, 56, 58; 69; 72; 75, 76; 79; 86; 89, 92; 130; 131; 137; 163; 171; 175

Brown, John, 38

Cambridge logicians, 198
Cameronian, 185
Causal connexion, between body and mind, 65–109; between surface and sense-datum, 144; 169; 172–5
Causal fact, 5
Causation, law of, and freewill, 110–31; certainty of, 112; compatible with first cause, 122
Change, 83, 84, 86–7
Character, 124
Characters, 22–31, 208–9
Clarity, 2
Cognising, 125; 135
Coherence, 190–4
Collins (and Drever), 43; 131
Complete cause, 118
Complete explanation, 67
Complete sentences, propositions and facts, 21; 196, 197
Completion of mentality in materiality and vice versa, 99–101, 107, 109
Component, 20–4
Condition, 67
Conditioned reflex, 80–2
Conditions of analysis, of perception, 138, 165; of truth, 186
Conscious, 11–15; 109; 125

INDEX